Christian Lacroix
On Fashion

Christian Lacroix
On Fashion

Texts by Christian Lacroix, Patrick Mauriès and Olivier Saillard
Photographs by Grégoire Alexandre

 Thames & Hudson

This book was published on the occasion of the exhibition
'Christian Lacroix : histoires de mode', at Les Arts Décoratifs,
Musée de la Mode et du Textile, Paris,
from 7 November 2007 to 20 April 2008.

Les Arts Décoratifs would like to give special thanks to
Christian Lacroix for his complete commitment to this project.

Les Arts Décoratifs

Hélène David-Weill, president
Sophie Durrleman, general director
Béatrice Salmon, museum director
Renata Cortinovis, development director

Olivier Saillard, exhibition curator and programme manager,
Musée de la Mode et du Textile, assisted by:
Véronique Belloir, assistant curator, Musée de la Mode et du Textile
Alexia Cheval, research assistant, Musée de la Mode et du Textile
Emmanuelle Garcin, textile conservator
Joséphine Pellas, museum textile conservator
Eric Pujalet-Plaà, assistant conservator, Musée de la Mode et du Textile
Myriam Teissier, events manager, Musée de la Mode et du Textile
Marlène van de Casteele, mannequin stylist

House of Christian Lacroix

Jean-Philippe Pons
Maud Kiener
Philippe Simon

Editorial co-ordination: Patrick Mauriès, Halima Millet
Photographs: Grégoire Alexandre
Set design with the assistance of Jean-Michel Bertin
Graphic design: Philippe Le Bihan

The clothes illustrated are taken from the collections of Les Arts Décoratifs
and the Union Française des Arts du Costume (UFAC),
as well as the archives of the House of Christian Lacroix.

Translated from the French *Christian Lacroix. Histoires de mode* by Ruth Sharman

First published in the United Kingdom in 2007 by
Thames & Hudson Ltd, 181A High Holborn, London WC1V 7QX

www.thamesandhudson.com

First published in 2008 in hardcover in the United States of America by
Thames & Hudson Inc., 500 Fifth Avenue, New York, New York 10110

thamesandhudsonusa.com

First published in paperback in 2008

Original edition © 2007 Les Arts Décoratifs, Paris
This edition © 2007 Thames & Hudson Ltd, London

All Rights Reserved. No part of this publication may be reproduced or transmitted in any form or
by any means, electronic or mechanical, including photocopy, recording or any other information
storage and retrieval system, without prior permission in writing from the publisher.
British Library Cataloguing-in-Publication Data
A catalogue record for this book is available from the British Library

Library of Congress Catalog Card Number 2007905204

ISBN: 978-0-500-28797-2
Printed and bound in Italy

Contents

Foreword

The history of fashion is like a long rail of hanging garments, fragile figures in a shadow play that tells the tale of the evolution of the clothes we wear. From his earliest childhood, Christian Lacroix has tamed these ghosts and now, to our great delight, he arranges the pleats and folds to form a personal history of fashion that is nevertheless an accurate one.

This couturier who once wanted to be a museum curator has become a fanciful reader of our collections, which he has enriched with his own unique skill. A different kind of historian, he knows the nuances of a 19th-century sleeve or the curves of a buttonhole that mark a piece of 20th-century fashion, however ephemeral. As the virtuoso designer that he is, he has turned this talent into a creation which honours a discipline that is forever creating its own future by reimagining its past.

With unusual care and attention, Christian Lacroix spent regular sessions in the archives of Les Arts Décoratifs, considering every garment, every costume, complete or incomplete, and every accessory in an inventory that boasts more than 130,000 items. With his characteristic freedom and generosity, he selected more than 400 pieces ranging from the 17th century to the present day, all of which are, to some degree, the sources of his own stylistic vocabulary. The work of anonymous or famous designers, haute couture or prêt-à-porter, work clothes or folk costumes, many of them never before exhibited, these clothes serve as a showcase and backdrop for designs by Lacroix himself, whose couture house is now celebrating its 20th anniversary.

In this history of fashion, Christian Lacroix turns his back on chronology and becomes a storyteller who is knowledgeable, mischievous and forever in love with this discipline that he understands so well.

It is my pleasure to thank the many donors, both famous and anonymous, particularly those who built up the collection of the Union Française des Arts du Costume, the fashion houses, designers and artists who, over the decades, have allowed our museum to become so richly stocked and influential. We hope that the scope and splendour of Christian Lacroix's work here will inspire a new generation of both couturiers and curators!

Béatrice Salmon

Inside the Collections

PATRICK MAURIÈS

THE CURATOR

He never became the curator that he once wanted to be (was it only a dream?). Instead, he was destined to be an inveterate innovator, a virtuoso of perpetual motion and constant invention, playing with the fragile fate of people and things like dead leaves in the wind, a fate which Cocteau, who knew all about that, saw as the very essence of fashion.

A strange change, we might think, (de)formed as we are by use and abuse, those diverse opposites, because to Christian Lacroix nothing is simple; instead it is complex, dual, apparently contradictory, dialectical.

A contrary curator, we might call him. And it is easy to understand why: omnivorous curiosity, false indolence, the desire to follow the thread of his own dreams, the fascination with the tricks and traps of memory, all of these things undoubtedly take precedence in him over the strict rules of an archivist, the need for method and historical structure.

He therefore excluded himself from that career, afterwards retaining just a little guilt, whether real or pretended, rather like a bad pupil who failed to finish his homework. But the student whose thesis on the historicism inherent in fashion history was literally left on the drawing board is apparently not that far away from the multifaceted artist and accomplished designer who can now look back on twenty years of relentless work and a career path that has taken him from fashion to graphics to set design to theatre costumes and interior furnishings, fuelled by an endless energy.

THE COLLAGE

If one were to succumb to the love of easy labels, Christian Lacroix could certainly be seen as the great couture historian, his work constantly drawing on historical forms and the echoes that they create. Although he often superstitiously protests his own naivety and the gaps in his knowledge, there are few fashion designers so familiar with the history of fashion, its arcana, its *corsi* and *ricorsi.*

It seems to me that revivals, transplants and juxtapositions give him an infinite sense of joy and a kind of dizziness, an almost chemical reaction that is powerfully creative, the pleasure of seeing history take on form and substance in a neverending chain of appropriations, inflections and transformations, of holding it in his hand in the form of a bodice or the curving lines of a piece of embroidery.

There are also few designers, even in spite of the above, less deluded than he is by the pretensions to masterly status and the claims of originality that the basic mythology of the 'modern' still tends to embrace. Nor are any of his contemporaries as aware as he is of what is currently happening, what is being created right now, without being blinded by the basic yet false opposition of 'past' and 'present', by the true path of creativity that is guided by modern market forces but which remains an intimate part of the design, texture and very nature of fashion. ('All art is contemporary art,' as an unsung hero of the 1930s once said.)

Free from all this dogma, he draws on all sources, all trends, all eras; he trims away or lets out (to borrow a sewing term) the detail in a historical garment, captures the memory of a texture, overlays one motif from the sixties or seventies with another, rummages around, like a child in an attic, inside the treasure chest of fashion and pulls out a shape at random, or even all of them, one by one. Just remember the childhood pleasure of cutting out, using scissors to carefully follow the outline of a shape, sticking it down, lining it up, pulling it off and sticking it down again, taking apart and then rebuilding a mixed-up imaginary creature, familiar and yet somehow new. Now think about the basic methods of collage itself, a crucial process in modern art and Christian Lacroix's technique of choice: looking at a newspaper or book, pausing over a detail, tearing out the page, isolating the shape or object, throwing it into relief, in a sense, waiting for it to spark off or fit into a set of associations, seeing it turn into a new combined object, a mosaic, with a dynamic of its own that redefines its raw materials; a hybrid enriched by a new graft that brings its older elements to life once again, letting them grow and flower into infinite new possibilities. It is always the object itself – what Francis Ponge called the *objeu* – that sets the rules, imposing a reality that goes beyond us and moves us. It is a form of *disordering.*

This, then, is one of Christian Lacroix's key techniques, a favourite modus operandi; a process that works like a chain reaction, a *mise en abyme*, the guiding line of his creative sensibility, opening fresh pathways into his artistic imagination. For this particular project, which is literally an *exhibition* of himself, this process simply had to become the guiding principle: a collage of collages, a branching point for new growth.

Thus the entire history of fashion lies behind Christian Lacroix's creations, as it might behind those of any designer, but rarely in such an acknowledged and reflexive way. However, this does not mean that his work is simply retrospective, a frozen homage, an obtuse fascination for the past just as it is. If we imagine this path through fashion as a personal museum, it becomes a projection or an explosion (not just a narcissistic continuation) of the self, of the designer's personality. No one is more aware than someone in tune with the Zeitgeist that the innate quality of memory is not to be retained but to be irremediably forgotten.

THE COLLECTION

The goal of a curator, in all senses of the word, is to create a collection, and Christian Lacroix's path is, in its own unique way, centred around collections, both of fashion and of things. Here is another of the tensions that he feeds on: although he may deny holding the status or rank of a collector (just as he makes light of his curator role), and shuns the meticulous valuation of objects, he remains a collector nonetheless, a *Spurrensicherer*: a gatherer of evidence. In his work we find – split or overlapping as always – the fundamental paradox of the collector: the desire to amass, embrace, keep everything and lose nothing, the affliction that the Germans still call *Sammeltrieb*, and at the same time its precise opposite: the act of framing, isolating something within a room or on a page, limiting it by definition. In this way he oscillates between a jubilant sense of plenitude, of simply *overflowing*, and the desire to refine, to select, to fetishize, to abstract an object against a neutral ground. There is no purer expression of the latter desire than the modern or modernist museum, keen to signal its opposition to the old-fashioned amassing of bric-a-brac.

I believe that Christian Lacroix understands that this unstable equilibrium within a collector can turned into a dynamic force, a creative principle. Haunted by the fear of loss, of seeing an opportunity pass by (and therefore the chance of a miraculous coming-together), he is constantly at risk of slipping into the land of might-have-beens, of suffocating under the weight of maybes and uncompleted works; stunned by the clutter that one might not expect of a fashion designer, a creature in perpetual motion who is always one step ahead of the times.

Within this apparent contradiction, he nevertheless finds what could be called the archivist impulse within contemporary art, which creates a dramatization, part empathic and part ironic, of the weight of time in the face of a culture obsessed with immediacy and pure presence. An example of this is the blind desire or relentless urge to gather up whatever remains of a moment in time, by some ever-shifting definition: Andy Warhol's time capsules, Daniel Spoerri's *Musée sentimental* or Joseph Cornell's shadow boxes: containers or assemblages with contents that are *there*, stored, assimilated, yet at the same time forgotten, simultaneously virtual and real.

A crucial factor in projects and installations of this kind is the heterogeneity and incongruousness of the gathered materials, and this quality can also be found in Lacroix's collections: a folk-art figure stands alongside a valuable piece of 18th-century embroidery, an antique engraving with a motif from the 1960s, a sophisticated photograph by Cecil Beaton with an example of contemporary brutalism. The crossing of registers, the combining of genres, the short-circuiting of cultures: these all place his concept of collecting in resolute, even militant opposition to any form of purism. Every object is partial by definition: a fragment, scrap or piece of rubbish – even in the form of a beautiful 17th-century doublet –

left on the sand by the tides of time, and it can only be given meaning by being placed into a mosaic, a new composition – a method as well as a means of exhibition – by the hand of a collector.

THE ARCHIVES

Our curator then found himself invited back into the museum environment that he himself chose to leave. He returned with a vengeance, with an idea in mind. This was the chance he had dreamed of, an opportunity to reshuffle the cards, to reawaken his ambivalent relationship with the institution and to apply his own methods, his own point of view and his own principles to a goal that was both captivating and daunting.

It began with an exhaustive visit to the archives. For some time already, the concept of the flipside or behind-the-scenes view of a museum had been a theme or chosen subject for countless installations, leading to a questioning of the status of art objects in themselves, their presentation, their conditions, their innate qualities, and more (Fred Wilson, Mark Dion, Joseph Kosuth). Museum archives are both a necessary place for conservation, the place where the machinery of the museum is hidden, and the building's own 'hell' or graveyard; an invisible, forbidden space, where decisions are made concerning the 'high' and the 'low', the major and the minor, the essential and the non-essential, what can be exhibited and what cannot, what fits the demands or the spirit of the time and what is alien to it. This space lends itself naturally to attempts at deconstruction and the questioning of founding principles, the nature of the museum and the nature of conservation.

Mining the Museum: Christian Lacroix could have easily borrowed this title from the famous project by Fred Wilson (Baltimore, 1992) and made it his own, playing on the multiple meanings of the expression: mining (even with explosives?), moving, unearthing the limits of the museum; extracting from many different seams; appropriating the contents of the storerooms he had spent months exploring, rummaging and cataloguing, and making them his own. Taking all the consequences from this: taking what has already been sorted and passing it through a new crucible.

This interweaving or re-imposition of order ties into one of his deepest inclinations: his historian's fascination for the way that fashions refer to and reflect each other, the way they are revived and developed over time, moving further and further away (like many creative forms, but in a very obvious and considered way, because it is the very basis of this 'art'). The distant is always being brought closer, in cycles that grow progressively shorter due to the commercial demands – demands for revivals that fit a schedule – of prêt-à-porter and haute couture. The thirty-year spaces between the recycling or reinterpretation of a theme that J. C. Flügel identified in *The Psychology of Clothes* have now been replaced by shorter gaps of five to ten years.

On a deeper level – because the motif is taken from his own imagination – Lacroix considers fashion to be an enormous chamber of echoes, a hall of mirrors with walls that come apart, recombine and reflect into infinity the details of one era within any other era (incidentally, this becomes the foundation, justification or alibi needed for his work with the collage technique).

It is not just the historian in him but also the fashion fan or fanatic who is fascinated by the way in which the dream – and rewriting – of antiquity from the Directoire period re-emerged two centuries later in the work of Paul Poiret, before being embodied once again in Dior, or for the nostalgic incarnation of the 18th century seen in the styles of the Second Empire, a secret source of the New Look and then unexpectedly revived by designers such as Vivienne Westwood or Lacroix himself; or finally by the relationship between the fluid, graphic lines of the 1920s and the lively theatrical adaptations produced by the boutique Biba in London, forty years later, which foreshadowed the multiple variations that can be seen today in the collections of Sonia Rykiel. And these are only a few examples of resurgences and revivals. A major figure in the fashion world for more than twenty years (and, we may imagine, lacking the necessary detachment to perceive the complex map of these territories and his own place within them), Lacroix nonetheless gazes over the entire landscape with surprising alacrity: annoyed to see himself associated with the 1980s, which he was not especially fond of, and with a lucid view of the stroboscopic nature of contemporary fashion: the way that the 2000s – because the spirit of the times is automatically sliced into decades – have turned back to the 1980s, just as the 1990s turned to the 1970s and the previous decade to the silhouette of the 1950s.

The Presentation

Confronting all of this, following the threads and ramifications, perhaps suggesting new ones, allowing ideas to cross and collide and engage in *accoppiamenti giudiziosi*: this is a ready-made basis for an exhibition. Immediately the next question is how the museum should present it, the objects that should be included, the methods of display that should be used, the logic that should be followed, the way that elements could be isolated or brought together. It becomes a matter of setting the museum in motion, rather as Hans Haacke did in Rotterdam (*Viewing Matters, Upstairs*, 1996), by extracting works stored in the archives and presenting them on partition boards, alongside more recognized works (or even masterworks). The fact that the subject matter is clothes – in themselves ranked as 'major' or 'minor', outstanding or not, iconic or simply representative – indirectly raises the issue of the nature of these objects: are they 'art' or 'decorative art', 'decorative art' or 'craft', 'craft' or 'technique': high or low culture? It can be seen how, as part of a generation, historically speaking, who wanted to give true status, in a semiotic sense, to forms of expression that were formerly considered to be sidelines or trivialities (advertising, photography, comic strips, fashion), Lacroix may have ended up choosing a stance that is deliberately distanced from the compensatory excesses and museum-style presentations with pretensions to knowingness, since clothes, as constructed objects, have no claims to the material and sensitive complexities that distinguish a work of art.

As someone who never felt at home with the frames, dichotomies and taxonomies that are the natural element of a curator, Lacroix found himself free to reshuffle the pack however he wanted – and, it must be stressed, at the invitation of the museum, which had chosen to become involved in this way. His choice was clear: instead of isolating, protecting and 'naturalizing' garments, fetishizing them, drawing them to attention, and thus conferring upon them the status and 'aura' of a work of art, he decided instead to remain faithful to his principles and to gather and accumulate, piling styles and eras on top of one another, filling display cases with as many examples as possible. The cases are not the hanging spaces that we are used to in modern museum layouts: they are multiplied, heaped up, linked together, with the clothes (as would happen with any type of work or object) immediately losing their status as unique pieces and becoming nothing but artefacts, images and relics from a long chain of moments. They might be the wardrobe of some immortal who has miraculously lived through all eras, or that of a family who have carefully stored everything over the course of generations.

From another point of view, this heavy mass of clothes, these tightly packed displays and these strange-looking mannequins awaken other associations and recall another form of close presentation: the kind shared by the 'temples of commerce' – an early name for department stores – since their first appearance in the 1860s, and by the temples of art, which emerged several decades earlier: the former displayed their goods just as the latter displayed their art: cluttered together in great profusion. By allowing his displays and his exhibition as a whole to follow this dense syntax, our contrary curator chooses to set the museum against the flow of the current, against the flow of history itself. Like Hans Haacke again, when he compiled a complete list of the owners of a painting, from the moment it first left the studio until it joined a museum collection. Or like a meticulous couturier, carefully unpicking the seams to show how things are constructed. Or like a collector, intoxicated by the chance to freely rearrange the elements of a collection that time has frozen and rendered invisible.

Christian Lacroix, in his own fashion

OLIVIER SAILLARD

'It's difficult to talk about my childhood. Perhaps an inventory would be easier: comfortable solitude, nostalgia, the pursuit of the past, endless trips to the Musée Arlaten, New Look skirts in Souleiado, festivals in Arles in the old theatre, bullfights as gripping as the voice of Maria Callas, which I listened to religiously, Dominguín and Ordoñez in the arena, Lucia Bose, Cocteau and Picasso in the crowd, the Rhône frozen over and the olive trees killed by the winter of 1955–56, the Camargue, Vaccarès and Les Saintes before the floods, white houses made of clay bricks, the dunes of the Lys valley, the *paso doble* in small arenas, the delights of Fontvieille, unchanged since the days of Daudet, and black-and-white television, the only link with fashion, along with *Elle*, a sacred treasure in those days.

A carnival atmosphere, the pilgrimage of the gypsies to Saintes-Maries-de-la-Mer, the statue of St Sarah draped in sparkling robes in the damp crypt, overheated by church candles, horse-drawn caravans and flamenco music, the natural elegance of the women of Arles in their traditional costumes, the beauty of the Place de la République with its town hall by Mansart.

The past, always the past: the splendour of Visconti's *The Leopard*, fashion albums from the era of Napoleon III found in the attic, dressing up.

This kaleidoscope of a childhood is very much present in this first signature collection, a homage to household gods, to my black-clad great-grandmother, eccentric grandfather, elegant grandmother!'[1]

In 1987, the year in which the house of Dior celebrated its fortieth anniversary, Christian Lacroix opened his own couture house and realized a childhood dream, that of emulating

---

1. Bernard Costa, 'Christian Lacroix, le grand "petit couturier" des couturiers', *La Croix,* 27 July 1987.

Dior himself, the renowned couturier of the avenue Montaigne, who died in 1957. In contrast to the greys and houndstooth checks that captivated the elegant women of the 1950s, Lacroix produced sun-soaked colours and never-before-seen combinations of materials and motifs of all kinds. The heir to a *salon de mode* culture acquired by studying the history of art and costume, he succeeded in making his own mark on the haute couture industry, in which the number of famous designers had remained static since 1973.

More than a couturier, Christian Lacroix considers himself a museum curator or costumier. His success as a fashion designer later confirmed his talent for theatre.

While a curator's skill at keeping inventory has certainly been apparent in his method of research and design for more than twenty years (he is a collector, amassing piles of cut-out images and souvenir stickers which become departure points for future collections), Christian Lacroix now devotes himself to both creating and cataloguing the fashion idiom that has become his own. Since 1987, there have been three successive creative periods that have marked the house of Lacroix.

The first of these, from 1987 to 1992, was the creation of a style that speaks of the south, in which the couturier's roots and imagination met his love for clashing periods of fashion history. The second phase, which began in Fall–Winter 1992–93, involved materials being silently damaged but without harming the haute couture archetype. This untouchable aura was what he later sought to destroy and drive towards the roughly drawn, free and abstract expression of ideas that followed his 1999–2000 collection and marked the start of his third period.

Christian Lacroix prefers to speak of 'before', rather than 'the past'. Yesterday might as well be a century ago. The history of the everyday excites him more than the worthy events recorded in history books. Copies of *La Mode illustrée* from 1860, found in his grandmother's attic in Arles; bound issues of *Marie-Claire* from the years 1937 to 1942, carefully preserved by his great aunt: these things satisfied his love of the domestic detail that is distilled within these magazines, creating pangs of nostalgia for a bygone age. Fascinated by an eccentric grandfather who instilled in him an indefinable sense of artistry and flamboyance, Christian Lacroix was just a boy when he first began to compile collages of the history of fashion, as well as producing his own sketches of the historical costumes worn by actors and actresses in films or plays that he had seen. He remembers the incongruity of Louis XVI costumes as depicted in illustrations from 1910, and the concept of filtering one era through another still captivates him today.

In 1963, Luchino Visconti's *The Leopard* intensified this insatiable love of costume and authenticity that seemed to predestine him for a career as a curator. Later, through the films of Joseph Losey, he grew to understand that a freer, less scrupulous evocation of an era, event or personality can be more emotionally charged than a faithful reconstruction alone.

An arts student at high school, who then graduated in art history from the Université Paul-Valéry in Montpellier, Christian Lacroix went to Paris to begin a masters degree at the Université de Paris-IV and also enrolled at the École du Louvre. His proposed subject for a masters thesis – 'The Study of Returning Fashions' – was rejected, however, in favour of 'Costume in Painting of the 17th Century'.

Françoise, his future wife, whom he met barely ten days after his arrival in Paris, and fashion were the two things that saw him through the boredom of university. He is able to describe her outfits as easily as others can recite from the classics: 'The day that we met in 1973, she wore navy and white wedge heels and white stockings under a wide peasant skirt with little flowers from Étamine, with a black t-shirt and a matching pearl necklace. Hair by Maniatis, blue-grey eyes, a Dior bag on her arm… The next day, on our first date, she wore a short Marc Bohan dress in stiff fabric…'

The couple shared a taste for fashion that could not be found in the magazines of the time. They loved combining new fashions and clothes from different eras, found in second-hand shops or army surplus stores, combined with unusual materials.

The discovery of a list of Karl Lagerfeld's sources of inspiration in a 1973 issue of *Vogue* strengthened the young Lacroix's convictions and also led him to build up a creative universe that he could make his own.

The job of curator slipped away from him, but it was at that time, through the support of Marie Rucky, director of Studio Berçot, that he had very encouraging meetings with Karl Lagerfeld and Pierre Bergé, in his capacity as a theatre director at the Athénée-Louis Jouvet, for theatre and opera costume design were still Lacroix's major interest.

It was Jean-Jacques Picart, whose new press office worked for Hermès, among others, who helped Christian Lacroix to get his first job in fashion. His time was divided between Picart's press office, where he worked as an assistant, and the Hermès design studio, where he learned about montage, planning a collection, choosing fabrics and the sculptural skills that are part of the couture craft.

From 1979 to 1980 he became assistant to Guy Paulin who had just launched his own label. From this brief journey, he retained the use of heavy leathers and linens, a palette of acid shades that can still be seen in his work, strong allusions to Vallauris, spicy colours, Roman sandals and ceramic jewelry made to match a range of sports clothing, from which he preserved only a liking for loose blouses. His sketches acquired a charming style of their own, one that they have never lost.

At Jun Ashida, he developed a more personal style, using the luxurious materials demanded by this Japanese house and then adding the finishing touches of Parisian style that it longed for.

Once more in the wake of Jean-Jacques Picart, who had been asked to gather designers' portfolios for Jean de Moüy, owner of the house of Jean Patou, Christian Lacroix became artistic director of Patou in 1981, succeeding Roy Gonzalès. He broke away from the 1930s and the Biarritz style that the house on the Rue Saint-Florentin was famed for, and introduced shimmering colours, flounces, embroidery, starched skirts and even the first bustles, which he shortened to miniskirt length. In his quest for improbable combinations, his first collection brought together a black top and a fuchsia pink polka-dot puffball skirt.

Red, white and black, those permanent fixtures in his palette, began to appear from his second collection onwards. Themes that would later recur in his work featured in the Spring–Summer 1985 haute couture collection (the Spanish collection) and in the Spring–

Summer 1986 collection (the so-called 'Circus' collection). Lacroix, who began to make runway appearances from the third collection onwards, shook expectations and attracted the attention of fashion editors. From 1986 on, they began to see him as an alchemist of different eras and the colourful prince that the Sleeping Beauty of haute couture had been waiting for. In the same year, he won the Golden Thimble award and in 1987, the CFDA award, which honoured him as the most influential designer of the moment.

He then decided to join forces with Jean-Jacques Picart and found his own couture house, with financial support from Bernard Arnault and later from the Falic group in 2005.

Keen to create a new style after his break with Patou, Christian Lacroix delved into sources of inspiration that were much more personal, including gypsies, jewelry, his grandparents, Las Ramblas, the festivals he loved in his youth. The tribute to his native Camargue region was obvious, and Lacroix's own folklore truly stretched its wings. In his new haute couture salons, at 73 Rue du Faubourg-Saint Honoré in Paris, the spirit of Provence could be felt everywhere. Along with it came short crinolines, tulip skirts, umbrellas and cloche hats, bustle dresses – at first thought outrageous, but soon imitated – and the women of Paris were soon beguiled. Red and black, the colours of the bull ring, mingled with turquoise and dusky pink and overthrew the traditional colour schemes of couture. 'At last, we see in haute couture the colours on the streets, the ones we see on TV.'[2]

Next to the exalted austerity of the Japanese designers, the monochrome of the Belgian school and the pastel shades of haute couture, Christian Lacroix's work seemed like a huge celebratory picnic, confetti tossed over gingham prints, and likely to survive long beyond the minimalism of the 1990s.

'Dressed in poncho skirts in spotted pony skin, black velvet spencers with heavy gold embroidery, the sparkling gypsies and *carmencitas* made the photographers crazier than toreadors. Their fingers started clicking while the fashion editors fanned themselves with their programmes.'[3]

At the age of 36, Christian Lacroix created a stunning collection, unanimously praised by the French and the US press, who turned him into a cover star like Monsieur Dior in his day. Beyond the carnival baroque and the local costumes of Arles, he created a silhouette that would become the blueprint for an era, based strictly on the opposition between a slender corseted bodice and a short voluminous skirt 'like an upside-down tulip'.[4]

From this starting point, making constant use of striking effects like mixed prints and gaudy colours, Christian Lacroix tweaked and adjusted a line that moved from trapeze to amazon. Accumulating historical and ethnic details is his favourite game, anticipating decades of fashion cross-fertilization.

After the overwhelming tidal wave created by his first collection, he moved away from the references to his native Arles and turned towards Vallauris on the French Riviera (Spring–Summer 1988 haute couture). Swimsuits in brushwork prints studded with shells

2. Bernard Costa, 'Christian Lacroix, le grand "petit couturier" des couturiers', *La Croix*, 27 July 1987.
3. Laurence Benaïm, 'Corrida baroque', *Le Monde,* 28 July 1987.
4. Marie Colmant and Pascaline Cuvelier, 'Deux ou trois choses que l'on voit d'elles', *Libération*, 18 March 1988.

nonchalantly moved down the runway like high-waisted paper cut-outs, and won him another Golden Thimble award.

With the Fall–Winter 1988–89 haute couture collection, Lacroix launched a challenge to the flowers, puffballs, frills and sparkle that had made him famous in less than three seasons. The look was long, haughty, intentionally enigmatic. Reliquary bags, crucifix jewelry and gem-studded boots created a Byzantine feel. His love of juxtaposition was in full effect. 'Lacroix's circus comes to town,' said *Le Monde* on 25 July 1989.[5] The fifth collection since July 1987 was a huge patchwork. Clothes were military or utilitarian in inspiration, drenched in gold; velvet and baroque stones filled the luxury salons. The runway show was not arranged in the usual order of day, afternoon, cocktail, evening. Instead, history alone was the guiding thread. The pomp of the Renaissance, the Roaring Twenties and the Swinging Sixties sealed the success of a collection in which both modest and decadent materials found their rightful place.

Gradually the runways began to fill with afternoons spent at the fleamarkets of London and Madrid. Specially woven fabrics for tight-fitting suits became de rigueur. Dresses followed the wild lines of the original sketches, with the poetry of chance being reworked through the craftsmanship of the atelier.

The haute couture collection for Fall–Winter 1991–92, one of the designer's favourites, was teeming with references, not least among them travelling gypsies. Guided by the gypsy caravans, Christian Lacroix revisited central Europe, so rich in bold, handworked embroidery.

The patchwork garb that he donned for a while, like some of his contemporaries, at the risk of typecasting himself as the 'jigsaw' designer, coincided with a second creative period.

Influenced by the theatre, for which he was also commissioned to produce work, Christian Lacroix began a process of organic deconstruction of garments which signalled a new working method and an approach that was unexpected from a haute couture atelier. He believed that worn fabrics, acid-stained velvets or rags could go hand in hand with the elegance of the corseted style.

This form of expression was reiterated in the collection for Fall–Winter 1996–97, in a style that was black and sombre, like the costumes he designed for a production of Shakespeare's *Othello*, directed by Anne Delbée.

The collection for Spring–Summer 1997 (another of Lacroix's favourites) was remarkable for the lightness of its lines and its delicate fabrics, which literally showed the flipside of this nimble-fingered craft. The guiding lines for this collection, his twentieth in haute couture, were dresses like water droplets, garments formed from iridescent threads and filaments, spider's webs. Rather than collage, Christian Lacroix turned to ripping and tearing, using rough edges, fringes and frayed hems at a time when minimalism was the leading fashion trend.

In Fall–Winter 1999–2000, Christian Lacroix went through a flamboyant divorce with the south of France, where he had learned his magical craft. This collection and the one that

---

5. Laurence Benaïm, 'Christian Lacroix fait son cirque', *Le Monde*, 25 July 1989.

followed formed a dividing line. Shapes became more abstract, less illustrative, and also less overt. Thirteen years after the opening of his couture house, the designer wiped away the over-obvious images of the Camargue region, a land that was now bereft of his mother, who had recently passed away.

While colours were used like accessories, they also became more violent. Neon yellow replaced sunflower, dusky rose turned to shocking pink. At the turn of the century, Christian Lacroix decided to learn the omnipresent techniques of information technology and abandoned his pencils in favour of a mouse. His onscreen sketches became cracked and torn, silhouettes were sharp and spiky. These digital designs retained only the bare bones of the past, of which Lacroix remains one of the few to possess the skill and vocabulary. 'Being a designer from the South simply means being Latin, reacting, thinking and working with memory, all those memories that lie just beneath the skin! It does not mean nostalgia, but a permanent connection with the past in everyday life…'[6]

The haute couture client now became a biker chick in leather trousers and brocade jacket, squeezed into quilted and zippered leather, her wardrobe laser-cut. She also enjoyed the couturier's oldest tricks, wearing an Arlésienne fichu scarf in white satin over a 'suit that in itself seems ready made' (Fall–Winter 2000–1). In the sourcebook of inspirations, art brut replaced naive painting, commonplace images replaced kitsch, surreality replaced scorn. The bridal gowns, those virtuoso masterpieces, sensational sculptures created for each runway show, grew in emotional stature and theatricality. Increasingly skilled at smoothly combining different epochs, Christian Lacroix reinvented one of Velázquez's Spanish infantas, topped with a black velvet headdress that took on the proportions of a Rastafarian hat (Fall–Winter 2001–2).

Through the runway shows held at the École des Beaux-Arts, the pretty faces of the girls were swathed in headdresses, which the couturier sometimes teamed with the nomadic charms of African-style robes (Spring–Summer 2002).

In 2003, Lacroix rediscovered delicacy and lightness, moving away from the Cubist collages that had vitalized his palette. He created a line made up of small corseted jackets with cutaway tails, from which sprung chiffon streamers and bulbous bustles (Spring–Summer 2003). A past master in the art of proliferation who knows every trick in the book, he used suggestions rather than outright statements, and rediscovered his bullfighters, his veiled gypsy girls and his obsession with the costume of the 18th century, adding an element of soul and shading to his designs.

'Much of the time, the past has a startling intensity that is lacking from many new designs. It's always a trampoline, a canvas, a springboard into the future, which, in the words of Goethe, is made from elements of the past. How could anyone imagine a garment that does not relate both to the body that wears it and to the memory that inhabits it? The past is the present in a state of perpetual change.'[7]

The couturier's much-lauded runway shows merge into a theatre of sensations. A heavily embroidered bolero worn like a piece of jewelry over a dress made from petals of flesh pink

6. Laurence Bénaïm, 'Christian Lacroix et ses villes imaginaires', *Le Monde,* 18 August 2000.
7. Interview with Olivier Saillard, 'Christian Lacroix', *La pensée de midi,* June 2000.

muslin (Fall–Winter 2003–4) signals the dissonant music of this alchemical designer and underlines the eternal nature of this inimitable expression of style.

When Christian Lacroix was a child, one of his favourite games was a set of cards divided into three (heads, bodies and legs), which could be mixed up into infinite combinations. He got as much pleasure from the thrill of happy coincidences as from the different kinds of costume that were depicted. He says he never stopped playing with this toy. This is how he learned his craft.

For the collection that celebrated twenty years of his couture house, far from the authenticity he sought as an adolescent, Lacroix escaped from fixed boundaries and displayed his artistry at manipulating the transitions between centuries, of which he knows the details of every decade, the evolutions in waists, buttonholes and sleeves. The articulation of a sketch or a gesture, rather than a mere posture, was the key to this collection of dramatic heroines caught up in a whirl of feathers and jet. Faithful to his obsessions, Christian Lacroix paid homage to Visconti's *The Leopard* in the soundtrack for the runway show, which began with the declaration: 'Everything must change in order for nothing to change.'

White

Of all colours, white is the one that is most alien to me, in spite of my fond memories of my grandmother who, after Easter, would wear nothing but white. It is rare for a snow-white dress to emerge from my couture ateliers. It always has a hint of gold, or bronze, or a creamy sheen that adds relief to the flatness, which seems too violent to me.

I often think of a line by Colette, spoken by Claudine in *Claudine in Paris*: 'Good God, white makes me perverse.' The immaculate wall of an apartment makes her want to throw a pot of ink.

All that white makes me want to do is create blots with my pen or with fabric. My bridal gowns, ever since the ones I designed for Patou, are sometimes ivory, often blue or red or gold; some even include black veils.

I never use white on its own: it often throws everything else into relief, a forced purity that hurts the eyes.

I prefer a black page or red page to a blank white page which gives me a sense of frustration, just as a dress in white fabric always seems unfinished to me. With the exception of the chic ladies in long broderie anglaise dresses on the beaches of Deauville in the late 19th and early 20th century, there is no period in the history of fashion in which I feel tempted by the sense of a break that white can create in a cycle.

24.
Haute Couture
Fall–Winter 2006–7
Model no. 19
Blouse in cream-coloured washed organza decorated with embroidered lace over a cream taffeta dress with a gold-sprigged organza overskirt.
Christian Lacroix Archives

Haute Couture
Spring–Summer 1990
Model no. 35: *Meringue*
Embroidered organdie smock dress with gold neckline over a tunic edged with white and gold embroidery.
Christian Lacroix Archives

LES ARTS DÉCORATIFS, MODE ET TEXTILE COLLECTION

26.
Cocktail dress
Jean Dessès, 1958–63
Finely pleated silk crêpe, trimmed with a broad bias-cut band.
UFAC collection, gift of Mlle Doro, 1978, inv. 78-27-1

Dress
Christian Dior by Gianfranco Ferré, Haute Couture Fall–Winter 1990–91
Beige silk crêpe with deep scoop neckline.
UFAC collection, gift of Christian Dior, 1993, inv. 93-21-3 AB

Dress
Christian Dior
Haute Couture Fall–Winter 1957
Silk faille, neckline decorated with ostrich feathers.
UFAC collection, gift of Mme Patricia Lopez-Willshaw, 1966, inv. 66-38-29

27.
Bustier dress
Anne-Marie Beretta, Summer 1984
Viscose and cotton satin, press studs covered in mother of pearl, broad flap of fabric backed with linen and draped in folds over the left shoulder, continuing as a train at the back, polyester lining.
Gift of Mme Anne-Marie Beretta, 2005, inv. 2005.32.112

28 & 29.
Day dress
1900–27
Silk charmeuse satin, guipure lace, tulle with passementerie pendants and tassels.
UFAC collection, gift of Mlle Nadia Boulanger, inv. 90-52-32

Dress
Mme Lucion Marlet, 1895–1900
Lawn embroidered with flowers and garlands in satin stitch, decorated with embroidered tulle and inset with white ribbon, shaped and printed chiné taffeta ribbon.
UFAC collection, gift of Mme Chancrin, 1986, inv. 86-39-4

Summer dress
c. 1900
Muslin with satin stitch embroidery, collar, bolero and sleeves embroidered with guipure.
UFAC collection, gift of Vredon, 1970, inv. 70-65-1 ABC

Two-piece summer dress
1890–1900
Linen, inset with bobbin lace, small frill of bobbin lace around the collar, ten mother-of-pearl buttons on the back.
Purchased, 1997, inv. 997.8.6.1-2

Garden-party dress
c. 1900
Cotton fabric, decorated with whitework embroidery and applied bobbin lace.
Gift of Mlle Liane Lehman, 2004, inv. 2004.231.3.1-2

Summer dress
1898–1900
Irish lace, flowers and leaves in passementerie, chiffon base.
UFAC collection, gift of M. Marcel Piccioni, 1970, inv. 70-38-6 AB

Dress
c. 1910
Cotton tulle, applied guipure lace, dress and jacket edged with a small frill of Valenciennes-style bobbin lace.
UFAC collection, gift of Mlle Pelle, 1950, inv. 50-26-1 and 2

Dress
c. 1900
Lawn, drawn-thread embroidery, applied bobbin lace, small frill of Valenciennes-style bobbin lace, satin ribbon bow.
UFAC collection, gift of Mme de Mercoyrol, inv. 96-07-22

Two-piece suit, jacket and dress
c. 1906–8
Ecru linen, broderie anglaise and applied guipure lace.
UFAC collection, gift of M. Dutilleul-Francœur, 1954, inv. 54-41-1 AB

Dress
1870–80
Cotton, decorated with broderie anglaise, pleated yoke edged with lace, pèlerine style.
UFAC collection, gift of Mme Léon Chancerel, 1966, inv. 66-14-2 AB

Two-piece summer dress
Thellier, c. 1900
Broderie anglaise and lace on a base of white chiffon.
UFAC collection, gift of M. Marcel Piccioni, 1970, inv. 70-38-7 AB

Girl's dress
c. 1910
Cotton muslin, bodice and lower skirt in broderie anglaise.
Gift of Mme S. Bureau, 1990, inv. 990.863

30.
Dress
c. 1910
White muslin on a foundation of pink pongee, inset yoke embroidered with satin-stitch flowers, light pink braid appliquéd in wavy and hatched patterns, edged with buttonhole stitch, small frills and modesty in ivory silk tulle.
UFAC collection, inventory control, unknown provenance, inv. 96-07-16

Summer dress
c. 1905
Linen decorated with broderie anglaise and satin stitch, Irish lace.
Gift of M. Al. Laidley, 1989, inv. 989.761

Dress
Madeleine de Rauch, 1939
White linen, buttons covered with the same fabric, initials 'HBC' embroidered in black on one of the applied pockets.
UFAC collection, gift of Mme Nicole Lefèvre and her daughter, Martine Allarousse, in memory of their mother and grandmother, Hélène Brès-Chouanard, through the intermediary of Mme Bernadette de La Salle, 1975, inv. 75-7-72

Colour

The fact that I am known as the 'colour couturier' has always been a source of surprise and amazement to me. Back in 1987, I took my colours straight out of the tubes without mixing them and loved the clashing results, even though they were criticized by fashion magazines and prevailing standards of good taste had always refused to accept them.

Colours, especially after 2000, began to gather dust, their shades bleached by the baking sun. I prefer champagnes, pale greys, sombre greens. Colourways shifted, like a book that had just been unearthed. All the coloured crêpes used by designers of the thirties and forties, virtuosos in the handling of the monochrome sculpting of the body, still enchant me today. As I make less use of pictorial or floral references, the colours that enrapture me most are the colours of fabrics, the colours of dresses that cannot always be found in nature, but which come straight out of the memory of fashion, in a sense, as if fashion culture had created a palette filtered through each decade. A sort of flower garden in Technicolor textiles.

When I was a child, my experience of colour was purely one of taste. I used to drink from the little pots of red, yellow and blue paint laid out by the teachers at nursery school. Later and in the same style, I used to choose ice cream flavours just to see the chocolate and strawberry together.

I remember getting very excited at the arrival of boxes of felt-tip pens, just as coloured pencils were starting to bore me. Arranged in sets of twenty-four, felt-tips enchanted me with their luminous pop-art qualities, fit for the coming 1970s. Perhaps that was the origin of my love of the prints of Emilio Pucci, whose legacy I was to continue and for whose daughter I designed several collections in the 1990s and 2000s. I remember how I used to enjoy jumbling up the coloured pen caps and then laying them out in order again.

However, I did not use much colour on paper and for a long time I was content to sketch in black and white.

One of my favourite things to do when I discovered Yves Saint Laurent's designs in magazines in 1975 was to find combinations that I loved, like red and orange or green and brown, which were considered taboo at the time.

My 'talent' as a colourist comes purely from research and hard work, collection after collection. It is born from a desire to reconcile the irreconcilable on a palette, even though some colours have very specific sources and identities. From my experience with Guy Paulin, who was a wonderful colourist, I have retained a taste for some quite specific colours, including chartreuse yellow, sang-de-boeuf red, sage green with a hint of yellow, paprika, saffron…

The red that I love to use everywhere, the red of churches, bullfights and fire engines, comes most of all from my mother: it was her favourite colour. She often dressed me in red, or at least with a touch of red, which had a cheering effect, especially when contrasted with a very bright yellow. It was from her that I got the habit of always having something red on me.

32.
Haute Couture
Spring–Summer 1995
Model no. 53
Long dress with bodice and train
in orange and deep pink satin over
a deep red sheath skirt.
Christian Lacroix Archives

Haute Couture
Spring–Summer 1999
Model no. 36
Bustier dress in black damask
with long skirt in emerald silk
and Japanese-style bow in pink
silk dupion on the front.
Christian Lacroix Archives

Haute Couture
Fall–Winter 2004–5
Model no. 38
Cape coat in coral taffeta gathered
with black ribbons over a flesh pink
dress in draped jersey organza and
chiffon, worked in graduating tones
and ruched.
Christian Lacroix Archives

35.
Squale **dress**
Carven, Winter 1952–53
Wool crêpe in petrol blue.
Purchased, 2005, inv. 2005.5.4

Day dress
Grès, c. 1947
Wool jersey in moss green.
Purchased, 2005, inv. 2005.5.7

Dress
Jeanne Lafaurie, Spring–Summer 1939
Silk crêpe in golden yellow.
Gift of Mme Annette Laurent, 1996, inv. 996.7.1

36.
Ball gown
Jean Dessès, 1958–63
Fuchsia duchesse satin.
Gift of Mme Kosciusko-Morizet, 1999, inv. 999.20.10

37.
Evening dress
Charles Frederick Worth, 1893-4
Orange gros de Tours brocade with white
feather motif, draped with ivory chiffon.
Gift of Mrs Franklin Gordon Dexter, 1920, inv. 22014.BG

Short cape
Jeanne Lanvin, Summer 1934
Bright red silk crêpe.
Gift of Mmes Henri Boitet, Jacqueline Goudard-Lacroix
and Martine Goudard, in memory of their mother,
Mme Félix Goudard, 1992, inv. 992.447

Evening dress and stole
Yves Saint Laurent,
Haute Couture Fall–Winter 1985–86
Pink satin covered with Chantilly lace,
lavender satin stole.
Gift of the house of Yves Saint Laurent, 1998, inv. 998.39.35

Dress
Jean Patou, 1935–39
Red organza on a red taffeta foundation.
UFAC collection, gift of M. Giraudeau-Drian, 1961, inv. 61-30-2

38 & 39.
Dress
c. 1920
Bright red panne
UFAC collection, inventory control, unknown provenance,
1986, inv. 86-07-147

Dress with train
Mme A. Mary, 1890–1900
Maroon velvet embroidered with beads
and sequins in matching tones.
UFAC collection, gift of Wittmann, 1964, inv. 64-9-2 AB

House coat
Cristobal Balenciaga, c. 1940
Silk velvet in garnet red and quilted
taffeta in dusky rose.
Gift of Mme Ludmilla Vlasto, 1983, inv. 53217

Two-piece dress
Mme Vve Lancelot, 1890–1900
Silk velvet in midnight blue with flounces
of crushed chiffon in purple and blue
and damask silk lining.
UFAC collection, gift of Mme Bouchot-Saupique, 1968,
inv. 68-2-2 AB

Long dress
Jeanne Paquin, 1930–35
Silk velvet in emerald green and
garnet red.
UFAC collection, gift of the Marchioness of Paris, 1971,
inv. 71-27-9 AB

40.
Dress
1922–25
Bronze silk jersey.
UFAC collection, gift of M. Marcel Piccioni, 1970, inv. 70-38-33

Evening dress and stole
Jeanne Lanvin, 1932
Brown crêpe de Chine and silk tulle,
edged with emerald green marabou,
lined with brown crêpe.
UFAC collection, purchased, 1992, inv. 92.17.1.AB

Jacket and skirt ensemble
Hanro, 1949–52
Wool jersey, pale blue jacket, chocolate
brown skirt.
Purchased, 2004, inv. 2004.7.38.1-3

Evening coat
Jenny, 1920
Quilted brown satin, brown
passementerie tassels, long sleeves
decorated with small buttons.
UFAC collection, gift of Mme Hélène Brès-Chouanard,
1975, inv. 75-7-93

Evening dress
Augustabernard, c. 1935
Dark green marocain, round neck,
four gilt buttons on the shoulder, small
gathered flounce at the hem of the skirt.
Purchased, 1992, inv. RI 2007.215.1

41.
Dress
Madeleine Vionnet, Summer 1939
Navy blue Rosalba crêpe.
UFAC collection, gift of Mme Madeleine Huot, 1976, inv. 76-39-1
Mme Huot's (dyed) wedding dress,
based on an evening dress
from the 1938 collection

Evening dress
Elsa Schiaparelli, 1930–35
Peacock blue and mauve silk taffeta.
UFAC collection, gift of Mme Elsa Schiaparelli, 1973, inv. 73-21-8

Stripes

Filling entire volumes of sample books, the motifs that produced the 'optical' dresses of the 19th century, stripes, fine or thick, are the sign of modernity in any decade, as was the case with the Courrèges stripes of the 1960s, which are far more interesting to me than his arctic white, for example.

Every haute couture season, we always select stripes from Taroni in a range of amazing sizes: they are true bringers of happiness. The same goes with Marescot embroidery; we always use up a whole sample book on a collection. Stripes give volume and three-dimensionality to a silhouette; they do more than make it look longer, as the tips in fashion magazines say.

When I was bored at school, I used to fill margins with parallel lines. I covered entire empty pages in my exercise book with rows and rows of lines, just for the sheer pleasure of filling up space.

I was also fascinated by engravers who created a sense of depth by using nothing but lines, without resorting to colour.

The stripes I love are not those of bathing costumes and sailor suits. They come to me from the character of Bécassine the Breton nurse, and the wallpapered rooms of her employer, the Marquise de Grand-Air, and also from Georges Lepape and Charles Rennie Mackintosh, and from flags and other strong graphic symbols.

When I was ten years old, I was allowed to choose the wallpaper for my bedroom and the furniture I wanted to have around me. I remember the Directoire-style striped fabric in salmon pink and off-white that was my chosen preference, the Regency bed, and most of all the desire to recreate the decor of a bygone era that I had never known and whose shapes I sketched in my carefully maintained notebooks.

The graphic qualities of the wide stripes of the eighties have now been replaced by roughly drawn stripes. Brushstroke irregularities applied with varying pressure add a certain clumsy quality, a sense of real life.

44.
Haute Couture
Fall–Winter 1987–88
Model no. 36: *Cigale*
Black lace dress with skirt of
black and white striped satin,
white lace trimmings and red
satin shawl.
Christian Lacroix Archives

Haute Couture
Fall–Winter 2002–3
Model no. 15
Cassock coat in black jersey,
backed with satin in wide ivory
and white stripes, with a red
satin tie detail.
Tunic in red Chantilly lace with
jabot of pale pink Chantilly lace.
Christian Lacroix Archives

46.
Two-piece dress: loose blouson top
and full skirt
1780–90
Pekin with black satin and bright pink
taffeta stripes, shaped bodice, lining of
ecru cotton, laced at the front.
UFAC collection, purchased, 1949, inv. 49-32-12 AB

47.
'Transformation dress': day bodices,
crinoline skirt with train, and
adjustable apron-effect overskirt
1868–72
Organdie with blue and white stripes,
white tulle, ribbon and buttons covered
in blue taffeta, applied lace, velvet ribbon
and blue taffeta band, crochet lace.
UFAC collection, gift of Mme Chancrin, 1986,
inv. 86-39-17 ABCDE

Two-piece dress, short boned bodice
and skirt
1870–75
Glazed percale with white and lilac
stripes, edged with flounces, buttons
covered in the same fabric.
UFAC collection, purchased, 1949, inv. UF 49-32-192 AB

Evening dress, boned bodice, skirt
with train, overskirt with bustle
1868–70
Gauze with wide stripes in white and
mauve, silk lace frill with crystal and
white beads, mauve ribbon, lined with
ecru glazed percale and white tarletan.
UFAC collection, gift of Mme Gabrielle Tessier, 1968, inv. 68-20-1

Evening dress, boned bodice,
evening bodice and crinoline skirt
Robes et Confections Mme Gabrielle
1869
White gauze with bright pink satin
stripes, satin bias in the same shade,
satin bow at the front, adjustable belt
with fringing in bright pink satin,
lined with cream taffeta.
UFAC collection, gift of M. Jacques Bonneau, 1949,
inv. UF 49-17-1 ABCD

Evening dress, boned bodice, skirt with
train, adjustable overskirt with bustle
1868–72
White gauze with pink satin stripes,
ruched pink satin, white lining.
UFAC collection, anonymous gift, 1987, inv. 87-07-8 ABC

Louis XV-style shepherdess costume,
bodice with pagoda sleeves and skirt
with panniers
1860–70
White faille, ruches of cherry red
satin and white lace, red bows on the
shoulders, false corseting at the front
in white taffeta with stripes of cherry
red satin.
UFAC collection, gift of M. and Mme Louis de Marcheville, 1950,
inv. 50-30-15 AB

48.
Two-piece dress: jacket-style long fitted
bodice and skirt with bustle
1870–80
Silk patterned with wide blue and white
stripes, long boned bodice, mother-
of-pearl buttons, white cotton lining,
crinoline skirt.
UFAC collection, purchased, 1949, inv. 49-32-191 AB

Dress
Dorothée Bis, 1970s
Bias-cut polyester, printed motif of
diagonal black stripes on a bright pink
ground.
UFAC collection, gift of Mme Véronique Monier, 1978,
inv. 78-41-15

Dress and stole
Claire McCardell Clothes by Townley,
c. 1953
Artificial shot silk with a woven pattern
of yellow, black, white and red stripes,
bias-cut in four sections and assembled
so that the stripes run counter to one
another.
Gift of Hood College, Frederick, Maryland, 2005,
inv. 2005.162.3.1-2

49.
Two-piece dress, long fitted bodice,
crinoline skirt
Vidal, 1870–75
Shot grey-blue faille, skirt and bodice
inset with ruffles and frills, apron-style
front made up of superimposed bands,
bodice lined with undyed cotton and
faille.
UFAC collection, gift of Mme Debray, 1954, inv. 54-64-4 AB

Spots

Twenty years ago, at a conference in Paris, a journalist was startled to see spots in a couture collection that I had designed for Jean Patou. 'Why spots? But why spots?' she kept asking. 'You still haven't explained the spots!' That was all she could think about. I don't think I ever gave her an answer. To me, Patou and the Rue Saint-Florentin were a way of rediscovering the spirit of Kiraz's cartoons of the 1960s, the designs of Michel Goma, the black and white of the 1930s, the summer seasons that moved from Paris to Biarritz via Deauville, the nautical look in navy, red and white, like the sailors' stripes on Bastille Day after the war. or the 'back to nature' look: wheat, daisies, cornflowers, poppies and gingham checks, or the New Look, with huge white hats for horseracing and polo (Judith Magre in *Les Amants*). Spots that were graphic, post-punk, oversized, like a form of fabric branding for Jean Patou. Patou and polka dots, the two simply went together like an ideogram, a tautology.

Moving even deeper into the storehouse of my memory, I find white dots on a black ground from the 1940s, the Occupation and its aftermath, Suzy Delair, Micheline Presle and Danielle Darrieux. Or my aunts from the Cévennes region in cotton satin, with a white collar, the sign of Mediterranean elegance for both rich and poor, or the chests of wealthy women where polka dots merged with strings of pearls, sometimes real, sometimes false. Tiny polka dots, the ones that 'looked good in every home', as the saying went.

Not to forget the stereotypical spots on the flamenco dresses of gypsy dolls in the windows of tobacconist's stores and on the chests of pilgrim gypsies, on the cinema screen at the peak of the Latin mambo and cha-cha-cha craze, on the shirts of the herdsmen of the Camargue, who did not yet dare adorn themselves with the Souleiado prints they wear today, on the petticoats of ladies who seemed to be made from circles: frills, hoop earrings, rosebud mouths, curving pencilled brows, the smoke rings of Carmen and the *Gitanes* gypsy girl on the blue packet; almost anywhere, upstairs or downstairs, varying only in size and colour.

Another factor was probably the effect of this supposedly perfect shape, in both hollow or filled form. I remember my very first nursery school scribbles, drawn in nothing but circles: lumps for the hands, a ball for the head, wheels for the feet, a bowl for the stomach, a bubble for the chest, a potato for the nose. Circles within circles, spots within spots, seeking shelter, hiding amid the multitude.

I don't know of any 18th-century spots. Perhaps in the early cotton fabrics of the 19th century? Spots were probably a peasant style to begin with, before they grew flirtatious in the works of Manet and Renoir, then became the banner of Toulouse-Lautrec's ladies of the night, the circuses and the cabarets, the cancan dancers (I used them a lot in the costumes for *La Gaieté Parisienne*). Then came the spots worn by Arletty in the movies *Hôtel du Nord* and *Fric-Frac*, Minnie Mouse – one of the first women in my life! – and *Didine the Rabbit* (one of my favourite comic strips as a child, along with *Riquiqui et Roudoudou* in the 1950s). In short, spots can be both gloved elegance and rustic charm, old-time and new-wave, a signal of sexiness and a sign of sickness; they are an illness, an addiction, an eruption, an inheritance, cloned and clownish.

CHRISTIAN LACROIX COLLECTION

52.
Haute Couture
Spring–Summer 2000
Model no. 34
'Jardinière' gown in sky blue faille with black spots slashed with a stripe of silver paint; ecru gauze apron decorated with naive embroidery and fastened with several transparent puffs.
Christian Lacroix Archives

55.
Haute Couture
Spring–Summer 2001
Model no. 1
Red crocodile skin jacket with rounded lower edges, embroidery and fringe.
Asymmetric dress in black crêpe with large white spots.
Christian Lacroix Archives

Haute Couture
Spring–Summer 1999
Model no. 33
Strappy dress in black jersey with a pattern of perforated spots on a red ground, Chantilly lace trim and large uneven flounce.
Christian Lacroix Archives

Haute Couture
Fall–Winter 1991–92
Model no. 30: *Pour une fois*
Asymmetric 'puff' dress in black faille with white spots.
Christian Lacroix Archives

56.
Haute Couture
Spring–Summer 2007
Model no. 3
Very short ruffled taffeta suit in black with white dots, decorated with black flowers.
Christian Lacroix Archives

LES ARTS DÉCORATIFS, MODE ET TEXTILE COLLECTION

57.
Belted dress
Guy Laroche, 1966–69
Double wool serge in ivory with regularly spaced gilded metal eyelets and plaited silk belt decorated with gilded glass beads.
Gift of Mme Hélène David-Weill, 1977, inv. 997.47.22.1-2

58 & 59.
Dressing gown
Jeanne Lanvin, Winter 1940–41
Black silk satin with white spots, shawl collar, cuffs and pockets all faced in red wool, belt with buckle.
UFAC collection, gift of Count Maurice de Ponton d'Amécourt, 1981, inv. 81-7-1 AB

Afternoon dress
1930–33
Artificial fibres, thick basketweave crêpe with a pattern of widely spaced spots, white on black, shallow V-neck.
UFAC collection, gift of Mme Hélène Brès-Chouanard, 1975, inv. 75-7-61

Two-piece dress
c. 1900
Red silk foulard patterned with white spots of varying sizes, beige and red lining, leg-of-mutton sleeves with small pleats on the forearms.
UFAC collection, gift of Mlle Andrée Frantz-Jourdain, 1963, inv. UF 63-12-168 AB

60.
Evening coat
Elsa Schiaparelli, Winter 1939
Façonné silk velvet, satin foundation, with motif of red dots on a black ground, black satin lining, red buttons decorated with metallic lace, imitation coat tails.
UFAC collection, gift of Mme Elsa Schiaparelli, 1973, inv. 73-21-22

Checks, Plaids & Tartans

Eccentric yet conservative, checks and their Scottish cousin, tartan, are the essential embodiment of British dandy chic.

To me they are also synonymous with the game of chequers, at which my grandfather was a true champion, to the extent of publishing books on tactics and techniques.

In the 1950s, checks meant my father's suit, tartan dressing gowns, slippers, curtains. All interior decoration had a taste of Scotland about it, and no living room was complete without a checkered drum converted into a bar!

As a child, I tried to have an image for every word. Checks were best illustrated by the aprons we wore at school. The nursery we went to tried to be different and got boys to play with dolls and girls to play with building sets. We also had to learn embroidery: I made a place mat with a pattern as complicated as a tartan.

While tartan is gentlemanly, checks are more rustic, and gingham even more so. I have always loved the picnic basket motif of red-and-white gingham: fresh on a girl, unusual on Brigitte Bardot's wedding dress by Esterel, more eccentric on a boy. For the last forty years I've always had two or three shirts in gingham or madras check.

62.
Haute Couture
Spring–Summer 1992
Model no. 18: *Tam-Tam*
Three-quarter-length coat in
hand-painted 'giant tartan' gauze
with straw-fringed collar.
Christian Lacroix Archives

Haute Couture
Fall–Winter 1991–92
Model no. 1: *Indulto*
Multicoloured hand-woven
tweed jacket.
Chocolate velvet polo shirt.
Brown gabardine trousers.
Christian Lacroix Archives

Haute Couture
Spring–Summer 1992
Model no. 56: *Je voudrais être en noir*
Bustier dress in hand-painted
'giant tartan' gauze
with straw-fringed bodice.
Christian Lacroix Archives

64.
Two-piece
Yohji Yamamoto, Fall–Winter 2003–4
Houndstooth wool with chiffon overlay,
edges left raw, fully boned hem.
Gift of the house of Yohji Yamamoto, 2006, inv. 2006.11.6.1-2

'Bump' dress
Comme des Garçons,
Spring–Summer 1997
Gingham print stretch jersey, roll of
padding covered in the same gingham
and sewn to circle the waist, high collar
Purchased, 2005, inv. 2005.7.4

65.
Travelling suit
Mme Siebenmann, 1895–1900
Fringed tartan, striped sateen lining.
UFAC collection, gift of Mlle Magniol, 1955, inv. 55-54-1 ABCD

66 & 67.
Dress
Mainbocher, 1930s
Tartan poplin embroidered with
scattered sequins.
UFAC collection, gift of Mme Patricia Lopez-Willshaw, 1966,
inv. 66-38-15 AB

Cape
Pierre Cardin, Haute Couture
Fall–Winter 1964–65
Checked wool serge with spherical
buttons.
Gift of Mlle Valentine Noble, in memory of Mme Jacqueline
Delubac, 2000, inv. 2000.2.111

Outfit originally belonging to
Mme Jacqueline Delubac

Cocktail dress
Grès, 1951
Checked organza.
Bought at auction, 1997, inv. 997.13.2

Skirt
Elsa Schiaparelli, 1950
Tartan faille with red the dominant
colour, flounces gathered at the back
to create a bustle effect.
UFAC collection, gift of Mme Elsa Schiaparelli, 1973, inv. 73-21-2

Evening dress
Yves Saint Laurent,
Fall–Winter 1979–80,
'Picasso' collection
Black silk velvet and diamond
patchwork in pale yellow and sky
blue satin, edged with black cord.
Gift of the house of Yves Saint Laurent, 1998, inv. 998.39.9.1

68.
Coat
Lanvin-Castillo, 1962–63
Bouclé-effect brown and black checked
wool with large black buttons.
UFAC collection, purchased, 1989, inv. 89-44-2

Skirt and top
Chanel, Spring–Summer 1959
Prince of Wales tweed and black
and white checked surah.
UFAC collection, gift of Mme Michèle Rosier, 1974,
inv. UF 74-33-15 ABC

Outfit originally belonging to
Mme Hélène Lazareff

Mixtures

Forbidden combinations of colours and patterns have always enchanted me, just like the gypsy women I used to see in Arles as a child. Their proud look, the way that they would freely mix a striped man's shirt with multicoloured scarves, their Spanish style never ceased to fascinate me.

Every May, there is a gypsy pilgrimage to Saintes-Maries-de-la-Mer, to celebrate the festival of St Sarah. It is traditional to hang capes and robes on the statue of the saint in overlapping layers. This creates spontaneous combinations of colours and patterns which may seem inspired although they are merely the result of chance. If I hadn't known they were originally Dutch, I might have sworn that Viktor & Rolf were from the Camargue, their 1999–2000 Fall–Winter collection looked so much like the statue of St Sarah. They dressed a single model in the entire collection, layer by layer, until she could hardly move.

The clashing combinations of spots, stripes and checks are also a direct reference to the extreme diversity of gypsy costumes. Maps divided into different geographical regions with dots and stripes, the graphic devices featured in my father's schoolbooks, are also not so far away from the free use that I make of mixed motifs. It was at a very late stage that I discovered Coco Chanel's 'gypsy' collection of 1939: it featured in one of the issues of *Marie-Claire* that one of my great-aunts had carefully collected and bound, and confirmed my theory that Spanish-inspired designs have been a constant in 20th-century fashion.

In the house's first collection in 1987, I wanted to create a dress in the image of that gypsy woman, a frightening figure, a stealer of chickens, but at the same time the most sublimely beautiful of girls.

‹ CHRISTIAN LACROIX COLLECTION – **Haute Couture Spring–Summer 1988. Model no. 55:** *Périchole.* Sailor top in black and white striped crêpe. Organza skirt with multicoloured flounces. Christian Lacroix Archives
Haute Couture Spring–Summer 2000. Model no. 37. Long sheath dress in a patchwork of multicoloured printed crêpe stiffened with white satin. Christian Lacroix Archives

Flowers

One response to the designer prints and handpainted motifs of the 1950s was the flower-strewn patterns that featured on my mother's petticoats.

I prefer the imaginary flowers of those dresses to the precision of a real-life botany book. I also love Napoleon III flowers, or the small, scattered floral prints of the 1940s, or the psychedelic blooms of the 1970s. I like flower motifs when they recall a particular era, be it 18th-century damask or 1920s embroidery.

All the house's haute couture collections feature flowers in great numbers: cut from fabric or woven into brocade, 1980s-inspired or 1940s-style.

For a long time, Arles remained scarred by the war. In partly destroyed blocks of houses there were walls with no ceilings, with the remains of floral wallpaper faded by the sun and weather. Sometimes the rain even unstuck the paper so that multiple motifs could be seen, to my very great pleasure.

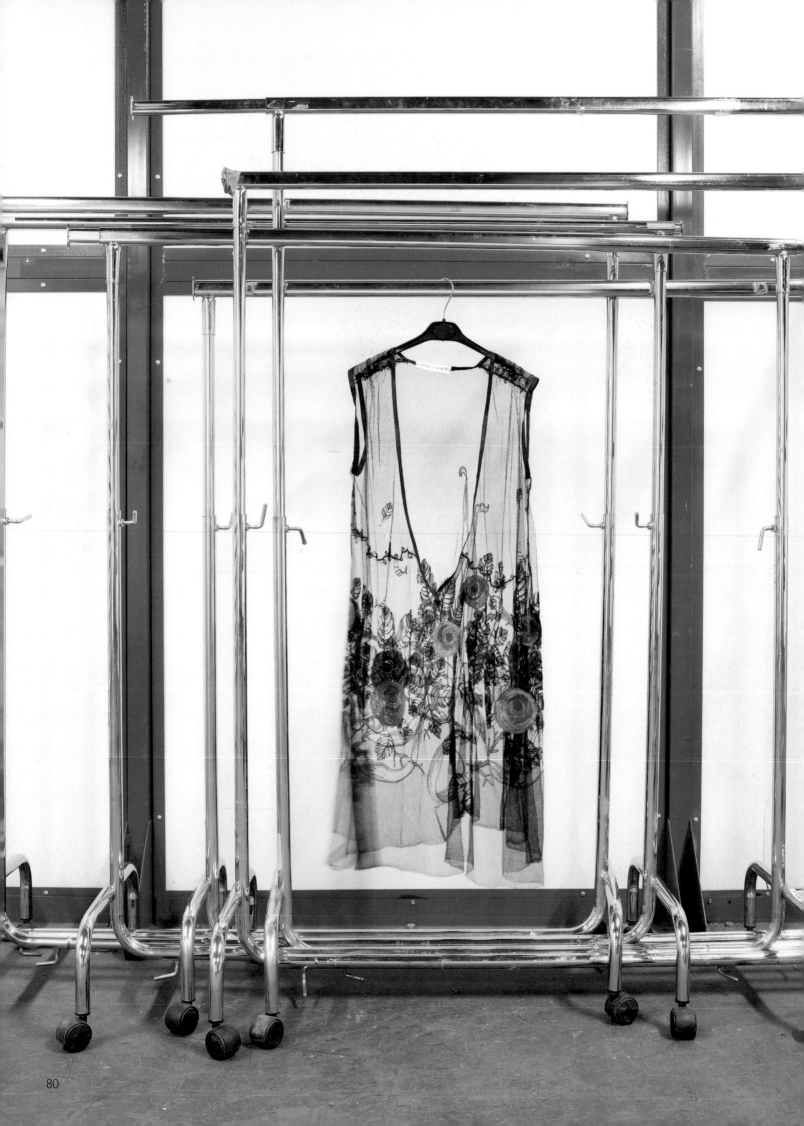

72.
Haute Couture
Fall–Winter 1992–93
Model no. 63:
Mademoiselle Hortensia
Ball gown in black satin with a raised
pattern of bronze hydrangea flowers,
with draped and boned bodice.
Christian Lacroix Archives

Haute Couture
Fall–Winter 1992–93
Model no. 64: *Victoria*
Ball gown in black satin with
multicoloured floral print,
embroidered girdle.
Christian Lacroix Archives

74.
Haute Couture
Spring–Summer 1989
Model no. 57: *Quand même*
Jacket in sky blue zibeline with
embroidery and long fringe.
Bustier dress in piqué with
Napoleon III floral print.
Christian Lacroix Archives

Haute Couture
Spring–Summer 2007
Model no. 38
Long dress with drawstring panniers
in floral print crushed taffeta, bodice
decorated with embroidered flowers
and floral taffeta bows.
Christian Lacroix Archives

Haute Couture
Spring–Summer 2003
Model no. 9
Short quilted coat in rose-pink
crushed cotton with floral print.
Short dress with corselet bodice
in pink and white striped satin
and pleated skirt in embroidered
pink organdie.
Christian Lacroix Archives

75.
Dress
Aux Trois Quartiers – Félix, 1908–10
Calico with green and fuchsia chintz
trim, ivory tulle, pink and green
cut-out flowers.
UFAC collection, purchased, 1992, inv. 92-17-4

Dress
Attributed to Jacques Heim, c. 1955
White cotton piqué decorated with
sprays of hand-painted flowers in mauve,
pink and green, draped jersey bodice in
matching shades.
UFAC collection, gift of the Countess of Montmorot,
1987, inv. 87-13-2

Two-piece dress
Maison Amélie, 1894–95
White muslin printed with sprigs of
jasmine outlined in black on a ground
of stylized flowers with four petals
and a red centre, small flounces of
Valenciennes lace and velvet trim.
UFAC collection, gift of M. Louis de Marcheville,
1949, inv. 49-26-13 AB

76 & 77.
Jacket
Rochas, 1930s
Black marocain, inset with layered black
and white muslin, decorated with naive
flower garlands in appliqué pastel crêpe.
UFAC collection, gift of Mme Julliard, 1957, 57-47-3

Afternoon dress
1928
Black marocain with triangular insets
in crêpe de Chine printed with
stylized flowers and leaves, chiefly
green and yellow, and wide yellow
georgette sleeves.
UFAC collection, gift of Mme Louise Janin, 1953, inv. UF 53-14-1

House coat
Patrick de Barentzen, c. 1970
Twilled wild silk with large stylized
brightly coloured floral print on
a black ground.
Bequest of M. Georges, in memory of the late Duchess of
Windsor, 1986, inv. 56964

Evening dress
Mainbocher, c. 1937
Black chiffon printed with white four-
petalled flowers, stems and leaves with
contrasting colour details and leaf motifs
embroidered in tiny gold sequins.
UFAC collection, gift of M. Main R. Bocher, 1961, inv. 61-19-25

Evening dress
Chanel, Haute Couture
Spring–Summer 1957
Black georgette printed with daisies,
clematis and lilac flowers in mauve and
pink with bright green leaves, bodice
edged with a garland of crumpled flowers
in the same fabric.
UFAC collection, gift of the house of Chanel, 1971, inv. 71-30-4

78 & 79.
Dress
Summer 1935
White seersucker printed with small
stylized flowers and leaves with navy
blue, red and black veins.
UFAC collection, gift of Mme Hélène Brès-Chouanard,
1975, inv. 75-7-66

Dress
c. 1935
Georgette printed with stylized sprays
of mimosa and carnations in white on a
navy ground.
UFAC collection, gift of M. Paul Walther, 1970, inv. 70-8-8

Dress
1930s
Silk pongee printed with stylized leaf
sprays in ivory and a scattering of red
leaves on a black ground.
UFAC collection, gift of Abbadie d'Arrast, 1977, inv. 77-29-8

Afternoon dress
c. 1930–35
Silk pongé printed with flowers and
leaves in ivory on a navy blue ground,
ivory pongé edging around the collar
and sleeve ends.
UFAC collection, gift of Mlle Nadia Boulanger,
inv. 90-52-15 AB

Evening dress
Molyneux, 1932
Muslin printed with a pattern of large
flowers and jagged leaves in black on a
white ground, Chantilly lace insertion
at the base of the skirt with appliquéd
petals in black muslin, black marocain
underdress.
UFAC collection, gift of Lady Duckham, 1955, inv. 55-58-1

Afternoon dress
1910s
Silk pongee printed with a pattern
of small white bellflowers.

UFAC collection, gift of Abbadie d'Arrast, 1977, inv. 77-29-43 AB

Dress
1950s
Silk crêpe printed with white flowers,
white cotton.

UFAC collection, gift of Mlle Nadia Boulanger, inv. 90-52-13 AB

Dress
Jeanne Lanvin, c. 1934
Silk crêpe printed with small black
flowers on an ivory ground.

UFAC collection, gift of Mlle Nadia Boulanger, inv. 90-52-17

Dress
c. 1930–35
Black silk crêpe printed with white
flowers and bows.

UFAC collection, gift of Mlle Nadia Boulanger,
inv. 90-52-14 AB

80.
Dress
Madeleine Vionnet, 1920
Black silk tulle with appliquéd black lace
leaves and a scattering of stylized 'Iribe'
roses embroidered in satin stitch in two
shades of pink silk.

UFAC collection, gift of Mme Madeleine Vionnet, 1952,
inv. 52-18-851

81.
Skirt
Charles Frederick Worth, c. 1890
Ivory silk faille decorated with bouquets
of flowers and ferns in taffeta, silk and
chenille appliqué and satin stitch, sequins
and glass beads.

Gift of Mme Franklin Gordon Dexter, 1920, inv. 22014.H

History

At the age of six, I got into the habit of carefully recording the slightest changes in the history of fashion, in the form of annotated sketches. I had a crazy desire to list every change to a buttonhole, every evolution of a sleeve. At a time when books on the history of fashion were hard to come by (I remember a book bound in purple cloth which I was given as a present, and which satisfied all my curiosity about clothes), I made a point of drawing and pinpointing all different types of clothing, historical and even traditional.

I wanted to be a costume designer before I became a couturier. Visconti's film *The Leopard* was a complete revelation in this respect. The meticulous care taken over the design of the costumes and sets was an inspiring example to me as a child and then as a teenager.

I was also fascinated by a picture at my grandparents' house (which I later stole to put in my own room), which was dated 1910 but showed a skating scene from 1790, because it compressed two eras into one.

Later, when I was studying art history at university and at the École du Louvre, it seemed obvious for me to write my thesis on 'returning fashions', but my proposed topic was rejected in favour of 'Costume in Painting of the 17th Century'.

Rather than one century in particular, it was the idea of change and alternation between one fashion and another that really excited me. The concept of being able to perceive a fashion trend in the one that came immediately before has continued to give me food for thought.

Historicism, the idea of using an historical period like a trademark, the ever-faster recycling of styles of the past throughout the 20th century: these are things that have guided and given structure to my work.

It is curious to think that Charles Frederick Worth, the inventor of haute couture in the late 19th century, also played a major part in the return of the crinoline which had its origins in the previous century.

Paul Poiret did away with corsets in the 1910s and created dresses with Empire or Directoire-style lines that recalled the great courtesans of the past. The gowns that made Jeanne Lanvin's name were those that seemed to boast panniers straight from the 18th century, and the ballgowns and cocktail dresses of Christian Dior in the 1950s were built around girdles that recalled the S-line of his mother's Belle Époque dresses. Vivienne Westwood's corsets and bustles in the 1990s, the 1940s-style collection by Yves Saint Laurent in 1971, the New Look revisited by Yohji Yamamoto in 1997: to me, all of these things are the catalysts of fashion.

The forward-looking/backward-looking nature of fashion is indisputable, although it is rarely mentioned, as one of the *raisons d'être* of a discipline that claims to be brand new every season. The 18th century viewed or reviewed through the eyes of the 1950s, the 1940s seen by the 1980s, the filter of one era over another: this is what I love, much more than some supposed authenticity to a decade that can no longer be verified, with every garment a hybrid, the costume of a costume.

84.
**Haute Couture
Fall–Winter 1996–97
Model no. 48**
Whalebone corset in hand-woven
moire in pale green with gold threads,
black organza undersleeves.
Close-fitting corkscrew skirt in shot
Razimir in lilac, with melon pink and
apricot underskirts.
Christian Lacroix Archives

87.
**Haute Couture
Fall–Winter 2003-4
Model no. 9**
Pourpoint in black faille decorated
with silver studs and ruffled sleeves.
Whalebone corset in decorated black
satin over a skirt of embroidered
black lace.
Christian Lacroix Archives

**Haute Couture
Spring–Summer 2002
Model no. 13**
Dress in off-white voile with black,
brown and green spencer-style
bodice in African linen and
18th-century silk, spotted plastron,
bustle and asymmetric shorts
with lace insertions, tied at the back
with black, white and red laces.
Christian Lacroix Archives

88.
**Two-piece dress: stiffened bodice, bustle
skirt, detachable polonaise overskirt
with puffed draperies at the back.
1870–75**
Grey-green shot silk with ruched
trimmings, bodice lined with beige
cotton.
UFAC collection, gift of M. Poulet, 1955, inv. 55-51-1 AB

89.
**Doll's dress: skirt and bodice
c. 1750**
Cut velvet, underdress in silver gros de
Tours lamé.
Purchased, 1887, inv. 3424.A-B

90 & 91.
**Dress
1902–3**
Holland linen with deep blue and
turquoise embroidery, high-necked
muslin tucker inset with white lace and
blue tulle edging, long bishop sleeves.
UFAC collection, gift of Mlle Densmore, 1961, inv. 61-11-1

**Two-piece suit
c. 1900**
Beige ribbed cotton piqué, collar
trimmed with linen in a blue and
yellow paisley print, black satin tie
with passementerie tassels.
UFAC collection, gift of Mlle Andrée Frantz-Jourdain,
1963, inv. 63-12-121 AB

**'Transformation dress': bustier, jacket,
skirt with train and crinoline
Soinard, 1865–68**
Blue faille trimmed with bias-cut
bands in blue satin and wool crêpe,
cream taffeta lining, corded waist.
UFAC collection, purchased, 1949, inv. 49-32-48 ABC

**Wedding dress
Blanchet et Murgier, 1882–89**
Edged satin with Japanese-style motifs
in yellow on an ivory ground, trimmed
with pale blue chiffon ruffles.
UFAC collection, gift of Mme Colette France Lanord and
Mlle Solange de Vaugiraud in memory of their mother, the
Marchioness of Vaugiraud, 1983, inv. 83-15-1

**Evening coat
Christian Dior, 1957**
18th-century gros de Tours silk,
silver brocade on a light blue ground,
blue crêpe de Chine lining.
UFAC collection, gift of Hely d'Oissel, 1963, inv. 63-11-1

92.
**Visite coat
Maison F.A. Lévi, 1880–90**
Brown velvet embroidered with a
network of bronze-coloured beads and
droplets, brown satin bows, brown silk
lining.
UFAC collection, gift of Mme J. Jomier, 1961, inv. 61-31-5

**Jacket
c. 1890**
Tan-coloured wool satin, leg-of-mutton
sleeves embroidered with jet beads, jacket
front edged with black ostrich feathers,
lining in pink and black striped taffeta.
UFAC collection, gift of Mme Clarens, 1970, inv. 70-60-13

**Sleeveless visite coat
1890–1900**
Black silk velvet, ready-made jet
trimmings, neckline edged with a ruffle
of Chantilly lace, dove grey satin lining.
UFAC collection, gift of Mlle de Lestrange, 1954, inv. 54-69-35 A

**Visite coat
1880–85**
Silk velvet in midnight blue trimmed
with ready-made beaded motifs in jet and
black silk braid on a black satin ground,
droplet beads and ruffles of Chantilly
lace, black satin lining.
UFAC collection, gift of Mlle de Lestrange, 1955, inv. UF 55-13 bis-3

**Short tippet cape
1890–1900**
Black taffeta covered with matching tulle,
blue wool appliqué embroidered with
jet and bugle beads, couched iridescent
metal twist and stem-stitched gold
thread, beaded fringes, small ruffles
of embroidered tulle.
Gift of Mme Tellier, 1996, inv. PR 996.13.1

**Short tippet cape
1895–1900**
Navy wool embroidered with black
braids on a ground of black satin
and golden beads, stand-up collar,
cream satin lining.
UFAC collection, gift of Mme Bettinger, 1949, inv. 49-20-4

**Short evening cape or pèlerine
1880–90**
Pink and grey shot silk, edged with
a ruched frill and closed at the neck with
a mauve velvet ribbon, black velvet belt.
UFAC collection, gift of the Baron de Curières de Castelnau,
1950, inv. 50-11-7

93.
Court dress: bodice, skirt and train
French Restauration (c. 1814–30)
Gros de Tours silk embroidered with
purl and sequins.
Purchased, 1991, inv. 991.76.ABC

94.
Junon **skirt, part of a costume**
Charles Frederick Worth, c. 1890
Cut silk velvet in moss green,
embroidered with beads, bugles and
sequins, train in yellow and orange satin
brocade lined with red velvet, frills and
bows in blue pekin.
UFAC collection, gift of M. and Mme Heim-Turcat,
1954, inv. 54-18-9 AB

Coat
1900
Beige wool, mother-of-pearl buttons,
lining of red and white shot silk.
UFAC collection, inventory control, unknown provenance,
1986, inv. 86-07-108

Ensemble: *saute-en-barque* **jacket,**
long-line bodice, overskirt
1870–75
Holland linen embroidered with braid
of the same ecru colour, long pagoda
sleeves, four Brandenburgs.
UFAC collection, purchase, 1949, inv. 49-32-193 ABC

95.
Two-piece dress
1882–92
Golden brown shot silk and speckled
brown gauze and velvet, large taffeta bow
with tassels on the bodice, lining in beige
linen.
UFAC collection, gift of Mme Honoré, 1988, inv. 88-13-2 AB

Cape
1840–45
Green and pink shot silk with check
motif, piped decoration of small circles
and flowers, green, yellow and pink
passementerie braid just below the
neckline, quilted lining in green and dove
grey taffeta with decorative stitching.
UFAC collection, gift of Mme Gabrielle Tessier, 1968, inv. 68-20-2

96 & 97.
Man's jacket
Late 16th–early 17th century
Silk knit in green and gold thread,
applied decorations.
Purchased, 1996, inv. 996.68.1

98.
Two-piece dress: stiffened bodice
and skirt with train
1898–1900
Dress made of 18th-century 'Dauphine'
fabric of silk and silver thread, white
tulle trimmings embroidered with silver
thread and floral decorations, facings
and frills, underdress in cream taffeta.
UFAC collection, gift of M. Marcel Piccioni, 1970, inv. 70-38-3 AB

99.
Long jacket
Attributed to Jacques Doucet, 1898–1900
Midnight blue silk velvet embroidered
with jet beads and sequins, pale pink
satin lining, leg-of-mutton sleeves,
stand-up collar.
UFAC collection, gift of Mlle Cléo Mérode, 1949, inv. 49-14-1

Visite coat
c. 1885
Red wool serge with appliqué gold
and silver twist, gold and silverwork
embroidery of Indian palm leaves,
chenille fringes decorated with red silk
and golden beads.
Gift of Mlle Laure Le Tellier, 1927, inv. 26002

100 & 101.
From left to right and top to bottom
Short tippet cape
Ernest Pasquier, c. 1885.
Black satin embroidered with jet beads,
high ruffled collar, edged with frills of
pleated and ruched chiffon, black satin
ribbon bows, silk lining.
UFAC collection, gift of Mme Pelpel, 1974, inv. 74-10-2

Short tippet cape
Worth, 1895–1900
Black silk velvet, large black satin bow,
applied black guipure lace, embroidered
with jet beads and black sequins,
flounces of black chiffon.
UFAC collection, gift of Mme Muller, 1958, inv. 58-39-1

Short tippet cape
1895–1900
Black taffeta covered with pleated black
gauze alternating with tulle embroidered
with jet beads, chiffon flounces, high
collar with crenellated edges.
UFAC collection, gift of the house of Chomet, 1965, inv. 65-18-1

Short tippet cape
1895–1900
Pleated chiffon flounces on a base
of black taffeta, applied decoration
of ready-made jet bead motifs.
Gift of Mme Arraud, 1980, inv. 48070

Short tippet cape
1895–1900
Black ottoman brocade embroidered
with jet beads, blounces of black lace
on a taffeta base with scalloped edges,
frill edged with jet pendants forming a
pèlerine collar.
UFAC collection, anonymous gift, 1950, inv. 50-1-1

Short tippet cape
Sineux et Cie, 1895–1900
Pleated black chiffon, black tulle yoke
embroidered with jet beads, black satin
bows and jet pendants, high collar
edged with pleated flounces of black
gauze and chiffon.
UFAC collection, gift of Mme Pierre Kernéïs, 1982, inv. 82-1-1

Visite coat
1870–80
Black cut façonné velvet, with semi-
circular motifs, edged with black braid
passementerie, raised collar, black silk
lining.
UFAC collection, gift of Mme Fortuny, 1951, inv. 51-14-4

Short tippet cape
1895–1900
Black satin with leaf decorations,
embroidered with jet beads and black
sequins, applied black net, high collar
edged with satin and chiffon frills, black
faille lining.
UFAC collection, gift of Mme Bettinger, 1949, inv. 49-20-3

Mantelet shawl
1850–70
Black silk velvet, embroidered with
black silk thread and jet beads, flounces
of black Puy lace, quilted lining in black
taffeta.
UFAC collection, gift of Général Jullien, 1955, inv. 55-37-2

Visite coat without sleeves
(probably removed)
1890–1900
Black silk velvet, applied ready-made
motifs with jet beads, collar frilled with
Chantilly lace, lining in dove grey satin.
UFAC collection, gift of Mlle de Lestrange, 1954, inv. 54-69-35 A

Ceremony

Church gilding, incense, draperies: these are the grandiose rituals that I love
to evoke in the bridal gowns that close every haute couture runway show.

Catechisms, churches, Easter mass: to me, all of this meant the elegance
of festival and ceremony, an event staged for everyone, like a theatrical
entertainment. Not very Catholic sentiments, all told.

I've also always loved reclining effigies, particularly the one of Bertrand du
Guesclin in Châteauneuf-de-Randon. The carved details of the stone costume
are often more intricate than those on a statue.

Bullfighting is another spectacle of the self, with the matador appearing
suddenly under the bright sky in a tight and glittering costume.

As a child, I had a head full of secret rituals, and I even made myself
a personal encyclopedia of my own rites and customs.

Every bridal gown, somewhere between the robes of a saint and a traditional
Neapolitan costume, seems to me to contain a trace of these vanished memories,
religious and superstitious, solemn and garish, mirage-like and forever fixed.

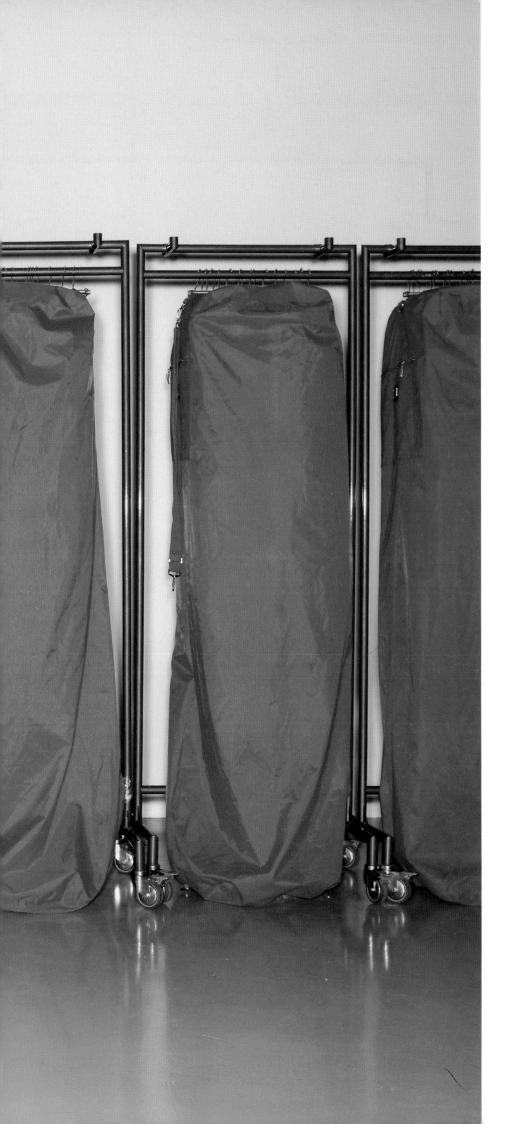

104.
Haute Couture
Fall–Winter 1987–88
Model no. 60: *Suerte*
Short black velvet jacket with 'ex
voto' embroidery.
Large 'meringue' skirt in ivory silk
damask.
Christian Lacroix Archives

106.
Haute Couture
Spring–Summer 2002
Model no. 39
Bridal gown in white tulle and
organdie embroidered with silver and
tied with a peacock blue satin sash.
Sky blue taffeta coat with bands
of gold lace; white lace veil.
Christian Lacroix Archives

107.
Haute Couture
Fall–Winter 2001–2
Model no. 27
Very short bustier dress in ivory
organza, decorated with a large-scale
lace motif embroidered with flowers
and ribbons; cascade of smoke-grey
organza forming a train.
Christian Lacroix Archives

Haute Couture
Fall–Winter 1988–99
Model no. 42: *Gold-Gotha*
Short jacket in black satin gabardine
embroidered with a Byzantine cross.
Dress in draped black muslin.
Christian Lacroix Archives

108 & 109.
Haute Couture
Fall–Winter 2002–3
Model no. 39
Bridal gown with bustier, overskirt
and skirt in embroidered flame-red
brocade, on a foundation of rose-pink
organza with metallic lace appliqué;
articulated gold sleeves.
Christian Lacroix Archives

Arlésienne

Since my first haute couture collection in 1987, Arles has been a theme, an inspiration, and its traditional costumes have been turned into fashion pieces, forming a leitmotif in all the runway shows.

By calling on my ancestry and returning to my origins, I let myself express everything that lies at the basis of my style and my way of building up the codes of meaning of a new fashion house.

Bullfighters, bodegas, the 1950s, the colour red: these were just some of the new deities in a pantheon that I wanted to make distinct from the one I had created at Patou several years previously.

Long skirts, the *chapelle* – a kind of shawl that goes over the shoulders, with seven pleats at the back, knotted at the front, a tucker and stomacher, the neckline turned over at the back – all of these elements that make up the traditional Arlésienne costume and the elegant arch of its silhouette are an integral part of the house's couture vocabulary. They follow the changing styles of the runway just as they formerly adapted to changes in fashion, like the bias cuts of the thirties or the flounced underskirts of the fifties.

< CHRISTIAN LACROIX COLLECTION – Haute Couture Spring–Summer 1988. Model no.17: *Pastourelle*. Jacket in Provençal print grosgrain. Bustier dress with umbrella skirt in Indian print cotton piqué, festoon print taffeta scarf. Christian Lacroix Archives.

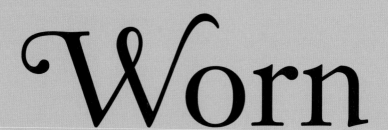 Worn

Worn like the robes of figures in a Nativity scene, taken out to be placed in a crib, dressed in ancient lace. Worn like the traditional dresses of Arles, the wedding gowns preserved by each family, the communion veils, the christening robes, all lying like effigies in the bottom of drawers.

In haute couture collections, it's not unusual to see an antique ribbon being used just as it is, instead of a new ribbon. It is chosen for its permanent creases, souvenirs of the box where it was stored for years and the hand that carefully placed it there. I am embarrassed by things that are too new. Old things, worn things, aged things have a living quality about them that is better than aerodynamic cut or artificial stretch.

The point at which I stop is when the dress that I am making starts to feel like it has already existed.

In the theatre, I dream of being able to make costumes out of other costumes, made for a different production. I like the concept of costume that extends beyond fashion, forming a thread that connects generation to generation, like chanting a magic spell, a challenge to mortality.

Dead materials, disintegrating under the weight of the years, allow you to see through to the other side, to the framework; a pattern is created through use and wear, an added layer of scars.

Fabric worn down to the threads. Holes and patches rather than new things. Sometimes we are moved to take an entire collection and make it aged and faded, coloured as if it came from a bygone age.

In Dickens's *Great Expectations*, there is a mad old lady, Miss Havisham, who wears the same silk wedding dress that she wore as a young woman, forever waiting for the bridegroom who never came. Every haute couture collection includes a long gown bearing the imprint of the past, a deliberate reference to Dickens.

CHRISTIAN LACROIX COLLECTION

112.
Haute Couture
Spring–Summer 2003
Model no. 10
Short jacket with flounced skirts in pink smocked silk, opened to show raw silk plastron.
Matching smocked silk skirt in graduating shades of pink.
Christian Lacroix Archives

114.
Haute Couture
Fall–Winter 2002–3
Model no. 18
Long coat in oatmeal tweed, embroidered with multicoloured paisley motifs in a rustic style, the long sleeves decorated with appliqué flowers in wool.
Christian Lacroix Archives

LES ARTS DÉCORATIFS, MODE ET TEXTILE COLLECTION

115.
Statue gown
1680–1720
Figured silk velvet on a silver lamé ground, edged with silver braid and lined with holland linen, bodice laced at the back, long sleeves fastening with eight sets of laces, skirt mounted on holland linen, with lateral bands of yellow silk.
UFAC collection, gift of M. Karl Lagerfeld, 1980, inv. 80-6-6
Virtually all the silver has now disappeared and the colours have faded, but an evocative sense of this lost beauty still remains.

116.
Long dress
c. 1938
Flower-printed white chiffon with a ruffle at the neck and shoulder line, full skirt and pink crêpe de Chine underdress.
UFAC collection, gift of Mme Hélène Brès-Chouanard, 1975, inv. 75-7-30 ABC
This silk fabric is exquisitely light and delicate and has deteriorated over time as the fibres have become dry and brittle.

Back to Front

The inside of some antique dresses, the charm of their intricate structure, worn by time, is something I love so much that some house designs are inspired by the reverse side of other garments.

The wrong side of a piece of embroidery can be applied just as it is to the skirt of a dress or the edge of a bodice, even a haute couture design.

The lines and curves of the raised seams turn necessity into a form of decoration, capable of infinite poetry and abstraction.

Another part of haute couture is the inclusion of a lining, an inner finishing to clothes which is just as vital as the outside but which only the client can feel against her body.

‹ CHRISTIAN LACROIX COLLECTION – **Haute Couture Spring–Summer 2003. Model no. 4.** Soft satin jacket with wide pink and white stripes, embroidered collar. Draped blouse in pastel spotted chiffon with a black polka-dot scarf. Very short skirt in black and white houndstooth satin chiffon, embroidered lace basque jacket in black and ecru. Christian Lacroix Archives.

Graphics

Around three or four hundred sketches, produced one after another, on several successive days, are the genesis of every haute couture collection.

Not all of them are retained. The ones that captivate me most are those in which the lines seem to be running away, in a sort of automatic process.

A lover of the hand-drawn motifs of the 1950s, I make sure that both planned and unplanned graphics are an everyday habit. Whether it is in the margins of a notebook or nowadays on a computer screen, I never go a day without sketching.

For a long time I enjoyed copying like a passive scribe any text that was given to me, for the sheer pleasure of seeing the lines form, following the upstrokes and downstrokes I learned at school.

My favourite silhouettes are those that resemble decorative initials more than sculpted shapes.

Every dress that passes along the runway during a show is to some degree an evocation of the increasingly abstract graphic design that preceded it. As it is being created, we follow the imprecisions of the line, the breaks and hesitations that are the mark of a hand-drawn sketch, the things that give it a pulse, its sense of opening and closure.

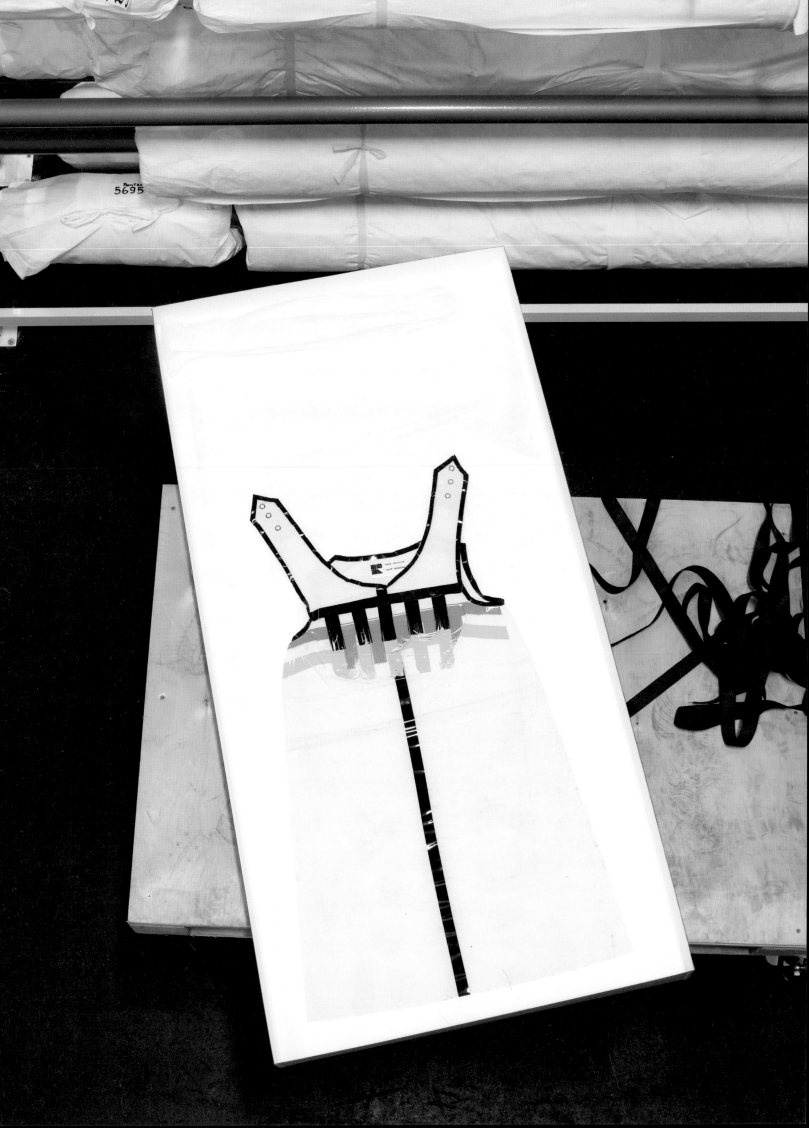

CHRISTIAN LACROIX COLLECTION

120.

**Haute Couture
Spring–Summer 2000
Model no. 18**

Short pleated, draped and gathered dress in organza with red stripes, opened to reveal a black tulle sheath with abstract flower appliqué decoration.

Christian Lacroix Archives

**Haute Couture
Fall–Winter 1999–2000
Model no. 34**

Long sheath dress in white crêpe with appliqué strips of black, aniseed, mauve, fuchsia and red crêpe, and removable cowl collar in black fur.

Christian Lacroix Archives

**Haute Couture
Spring–Summer 2005
Model no. 1**

Short trench coat in white duchesse satin spattered with fuchsia and violet, with green highlights.
Organza and muslin gown with large jabot neckline and gathered skirt.

Christian Lacroix Archives

LES ARTS DÉCORATIFS, MODE ET TEXTILE COLLECTION

122.

**Suit jacket
1935–38**

Ecru wild silk with navy piping and round navy buttons, straight skirt with slit.

Purchased, 2004, inv. 2004.7.73.1-2

**Dress
c. 1937**

Pink wool jersey with navy wool piping and navy resin buttons.

Purchased, 2004, inv. 2004.7.20.1-2

123.

**Dress
Louis Féraud, 1970**

Silk jersey handpainted with large multicoloured geometric motifs.

Gift of the house of Louis Féraud, 1997, inv. 997.67.4

**Evening dress
Pierre Cardin, 1970**

Double gabardine in fluorescent yellow Qiana edged with white.

UFAC collection, gift of DuPont de Nemours, 1972, inv. 72-26-4

124 & 125.

**Bustier dress
c. 1935**

Black chiffon edged with glossy satin ribbon in aniseed green and white.

UFAC collection, anonymous gift, 1991, inv. 91-25-5

**Tunic
1920s**

Cornflower blue silk crêpe and indigo cotton velvet.

Gift of Mme Jean R. Chalon, 1975, inv. 45204.AB

**Dress and matching coat
Callot Sœurs, 1924–25**

White silk grosgrain and black wool, mother-of-pearl buttons, black wool bodice with white stitching, white lace modesty.

UFAC collection, gift of Mme Nicole Lefèvre and her daughter, Martine Allarousse, in memory of their mother and grandmother, Hélène Brès-Chouanard, through the intermediary of Mme Bernadette de La Salle, 1975, inv. 75-7-40 AB

**Evening dress
Rochas, 1937**

Blue crêpe romain, belt in orange and yellow crêpe.

UFAC collection, gift of Mme Julliard, inv. 57-47-2

126.

**Cocktail dress
Balenciaga, Fall–Winter 1952–53, fabric by Lamarre**

Needle-pleated organdie, plain black body, patchwork skirt composed of alternating black and white triangles, half slip in black faille, hem stiffened with horsehair.

Inventory control, unknown provenance, inv. RI 2007.216.1-3

**Coat
Emanuel Ungaro, Fall–Winter 1969–70**

Triple gabardine with 'paintbrush' print of horizontal stripes in pink, orange and black on white against a plain black ground.

Gift of Mlle Vanessa Van Zuylen Van Nyevelt Van De Haar, 1998, inv. 998.208.1

**Dress and matching coat
Emanuel Ungaro, Haute Couture
Fall–Winter 1969, fabric by Nattier**

Wool with 'paintbrush' print of wavy stripes in fuchsia, orange and red on white.

Gift of Mme Hélène David-Weill, 1997, inv. 997.47.6.1-2

127.

**Dress
Paco Rabanne, 1960–65**

Corrugated paper and white nylon, geometric design in glossy black, orange and yellow paper that has been fringed and glued.

Purchased, 2004, inv. 2004.7.79

Lamé

Whether it is gold or silver, lamé is fascinating. It turns metallic thread into something supple and even silky. Sculpting the body, it is fluid and versatile, and the history of fashion is studded with its sparkling brilliance.

Empire dresses combined the white of high-waisted chemises with golden stripes or scattered motifs, forming a pointillist canvas. I know of no other costumes of the 19th century that reach such heights of magnificence, with the exception of liturgical robes which were often cut from 18th-century fabrics.

In the 1930s, Jeanne Lanvin was a specialist in evening dresses matched with small lamé capes that were often decorated with quilting or studs. All the couture houses of that era made use of gold leaf. Evening gowns with subtly elegant trains seemed like substitutes for the metallic armour of ancient times. The singer and socialite Suzy Solidor was the most striking image of a gold-clad woman. In the 1960s, it was of course Paco Rabanne who created a lamé revival by using real metal plates in his dresses, turning them into fashion gems.

In 1978, Thierry Mugler surprised everyone with a collection of long dresses with scales and fins in gold lamé. They became a sensation, bringing spectacle and theatricality into fashion and anticipating the 1980s. Yves Saint Laurent's sheath dresses wrapped the body with the simplicity of a jacket; in monochrome lamé or leopardskin damask, they sparkled in a decade in which fashion was once again in fashion.

I love lamé, this shining length of light cut from a roll to make a dress, glittering and new or worn down by time. Once the prerogative of royalty until it was democratized by the elegant gowns of the 20th century, gold is also among the colours and motifs that are rather harshly judged by fashion history, connected as it was with the overly showy chic of goodtime girls before it become more respectably associated with a handful of eccentrics.

Perhaps rather unconvincingly, the age of tinfoil wrappings and chocolate-box theatrics is now being reborn to some extent from those golden ashes, surfing on the wave of the eighties revival. Lamé is not easy: it is hard work, the metal twisting and turning rusty, depriving us of its former glory.
One thinks of a piece by the poet Mireille Havet in which she evokes the acrid scent of metal in the early hours of an August morning in the 1920s, when the shady nightclubs were closing up and sending home the aristocratic Amazons in their metallic gowns. Any gold and glitter that followed Poiret's 1002nd Night might seem rather vulgar to us, but those years nonetheless gave us molten gold, glossy or matte like a relic of Pompeii, against the skin of black models, the pleated crêpes of Anne-Marie Beretta, the scandals of *Dallas* and *Dynasty* and their comeback in the work of Viktor & Rolf or Jeremy Scott.

CHRISTIAN LACROIX COLLECTION

130.
Haute Couture Fall–Winter 1998–99
Model no. 45
Long sheath dress in aged
Chantilly lace with gold embroidery
on the bodice.
Christian Lacroix Archives

LES ARTS DÉCORATIFS, MODE ET TEXTILE COLLECTION

133.
Cape
Elsa Schiaparelli, 1930–39
Ribbed silver lamé, brooch
in silver-plated metal.
UFAC collection, purchased, 1962, inv. 62-8-19

Evening jacket
Jeanne Lanvin, 1938
Ivory crêpe, cap sleeves in quilted
silver lamé.
UFAC collection, gift of Générale Buat, 1954, inv. 54-8-6

134 & 135.
Evening dress
c. 1925
Lilac chiffon embroidered with silver
sequins, neckline edged with pink tulle.
UFAC collection, inventory control, unknown provenance,
inv. 2000-07-2

Jacket
Jeanne Lanvin, 1930s
Silk tulle embroidered all over
with silver sequins.
UFAC collection, gift of Mlle Nadia Boulanger, inv. 90-52-9

136.
Evening coat
Jeanne Lanvin, 1930s
Gold lamé with decorative pink silk
stitching.
UFAC collection, purchase, 1962, inv. 62-8-17

Sculpted Shells

What we notice about a distant silhouette is its volume, the outline that a skirt draws in space, the width of the sleeves, like a paper cut-out.

There is a stage in the construction of a collection which involves arranging fabric samples on the paper prototype of a dress. An artificial silhouette takes shape, one that is closer to the sketch than the final garment.

Like the cloaks or robes worn by statues of the Virgin Mary, clothes can harden until they become almost monolithic. This was the case with the design *Picador* in 1987; its quilted overskirt recalled the decorated textiles worn by horses in bullfights.

Dresses can be sculptures too, supporting the body more than the body supports them. This is true of the antique outfits of the 17th and 18th centuries, and it is also true of the dresses and short coats in heavy jersey of the sixties.

Out of a love of these full shapes, this architecture of paper and fabric, I try to make each design as faithful as possible to its original sketch, even to the point of deformation.

16.02.T.00

138.
Haute Couture
Spring–Summer 1999
Model no. 11
Fitted t-shirt in black crêpe with
pierced decoration along the seams.
Gathered skirt with oversized pleats
in white organza with grey edging.
Christian Lacroix Archives

140.
Haute Couture
Fall–Winter 1987–88
Model no. 48: *Feria*
Short jacket in black velvet embroidered
with Camargue-style motifs.
Long 'carapace' skirt in a patchwork
of blood-red dupion, moire and
taffeta.
Christian Lacroix Archives

141.
Dress
Christian Dior by Marc Bohan,
Spring–Summer 1969,
embroidery by Judith Barbier
Double gabardine in white wool,
embroidered with applied black and
white Rhodoid.
Gift of Mme Hélène David-Weill, 1997, inv. 997.47.19

Dress
Christian Dior by Marc Bohan,
Spring–Summer 1969
Double serge in white wool, embroidered
with metallic sequins, multicoloured
beads and green paste gemstones, edged
with black sequins and beads, lavender
satin ribbon.
Bequest of M. Georges, in memory of the late Duchess of
Windsor, 1986, inv. 56959

142 & 143.
Evening coat
André Courrèges, 1960s
Grosgrain, large buttons in black silk
passementerie.
Gift of Mme Philippe Castro, 1990, inv. 990.824

Cocktail dress and matching bolero
Pierre Balmain, 1966
Double-sided silk serge in cerise and
black, machine pleats embroidered
with jet beads.
UFAC collection, gift of M. and Mme Gérard Franck,
1990, inv. 90-59-6 AB

Cocktail dress and matching bolero
Pierre Balmain, 1966
Double-sided silk serge in cerise and
black, machine pleats, black braid,
embroidered collar of faceted black
beads, flat bow.
UFAC collection, gift of Mme Antoine Gridel, 1984,
inv. 84-30-1 AB

Evening coat
Jacques Heim, 1950–55
Alpaca with vertical stitching
and box pleats.
UFAC collection, gift of M. Alexis Noël, 1971, inv. 71-58-38

144.
'Normandie' ensemble: jacket, stole
and straight skirt
Christian Dior, Spring–Summer 1957
Mottled grey wool serge with black
corozo buttons.
UFAC collection, gift of M. Alexis Noël, 1971, inv. 71-58-24 ABC

Fitted coat
Lucien Lelong, c. 1947
Petersham in mottled sand and grey,
grey silk lining with a woven repeat
motif of the designer's name and address
('Lucien Lelong, 6 Avenue Matignon').
UFAC collection, gift of Mme Maurice Goudeket,
1970, inv. 70-10-2

145.
'Historiette' dress
Christian Dior, Fall–Winter 1955
Red silk faille, white tulle underdress
with boned bodice.
UFAC collection, gift of Mme Michèle Rosier, 1974,
inv. 74-33-14 AB

Dress worn by Mme Hélène Lazareff

Patchwork

Patchworks of fabrics, materials and colours, but also of times and places, of rich and poor.

A patchwork of skills has built up the history of haute couture, with the arrival in waves of craftsmen and women from Eastern Europe, then from Scandinavia and more recently from Britain.

From my earliest collections at Jean Patou, patchwork has been a perennial. The breaking down of a dress into its elements, pixels laid side by side, a series of metamorphoses, from dress into dress into dress, mutating constantly into something new, and never dying.

Cutting down, cutting up, recombining. From the patchwork jacket that an assistant discovered in a market and which became a uniform for me for a while, to the dress with a skirt made up of leftover pieces of fabric from different collections. Patchwork goes beyond fashion, drawing a new outline for a garment that is more nomadic than sedentary.

For a long time, long before fashion houses became truly aware of their own heritage and began to keep archives of their own designs, it was customary to work and rework a dress that had not been sold, adding a fabric panel here, removing a strap there, until it looked convincing enough to sell.

Britain, which has developed an knowingly kitsch side to its culture alongside its tradition of craftsmanship, is a constant source of observation. Both there and in the US, patchwork has become an activity as well as an art, a practice and a way of seeing in which both the ordinary and the extraordinary are shown to their full effect through a spontaneous or planned act of juxtaposition.

148.
**Haute Couture
Spring–Summer 2002
Model no. 29**
Patchwork gown with cutaway armholes.
Blue-grey organza top with silver
embroidery, balloon skirt with frills
in guipure, lace and cotton,
and red satin trim.
Christian Lacroix Archives

**Haute Couture
Fall–Winter 2000–1
Model no. 9**
Coat made from a patchwork of
parkas and bomber jackets with
a multicoloured frill collar.
Christian Lacroix Archives

**Haute Couture
Fall–Winter 2000–1
Model no. 40**
Gown with long-line platinum-coloured
bodice, embroidered with gold and
paste gemstones.
Skirt with heavy pleats in quilted
multicolour patchwork.
Christian Lacroix Archives

150.
**Dress
Madeleine Vionnet, Summer 1939**
Twill with a print motif of heads in hats.
UFAC collection, gift of Mme Hélène Brès-Chouanard, 1975,
inv. 75-7-60 AB

**Evening dress
Elsa Schiaparelli, Summer 1937**
Printed satin, draped and bias-cut.
UFAC collection, gift of Mme Patricia Lopez-Willshaw, 1966,
inv. 66-38-4 AB

**Short jacket
Elsa Schiaparelli, Summer 1938,
'Pagan' collection**
Black rippled silk with pink French
moire facings and enamelled metal
dragonflies, bee and mayflies attached to
the collar, pink crêpe de Chine lining.
UFAC collection, gift of Mme Elsa Schiaparelli, 1973, inv. 73-21-70

151.
**Visite coat
1885–90**
Silk velvet, braiding, chenille and thread
fringing, pendants and Brandenburgs
in silk passementerie, small tulle collar
embroidered with golden metallic beads,
satin lining.
UFAC collection, gift of Mlle de Lestrange, 1953, inv. 55-13-1

**Evening gown
Elsa Schiaparelli, Winter 1939**
Façonné velvet on a satin base.
UFAC collection, gift of Mme Elsa Schiaparelli, 1973, inv. UF 73-21-5

152 & 153.
Left:
**Short tippet cape
Céline and Fanny Liévin,
Paris, 1895–1900**
Black lace, purple velvet, appliquéd
braid and jet fringes, jet embroidery,
collar in the form of a large black
chiffon ruff, black poult-de-soie lining.
Gift of Mlle de Lestrange, 1955, inv. UF55-13 bis-2

Right, from top to bottom
and left to right:
**Dress
Christiane Bailly, Summer 1966**
Cotton with batik print.
UFAC collection, gift of Mme Christiane Bailly, 1984, inv. 84-37-4

**Summer dress
1912–14**
Silk tulle with appliqué of broderie
anglaise and paisley print muslin.
UFAC collection, gift of Mme Clarens, 1970, inv. 70-60-1

**Dress
Lucien Lelong, c. 1938**
Goffered silk crêpe, navy ground
with a repeat motif of white matches
with blue and red tips scattered
around a box of matches marked
with the couturier's initials.
UFAC collection, gift of Mme Paul Walther, 1970, inv. 70-8-3

**Visite coat
1870–90**
Cut from a cashmere shawl,
with fringes, braid, pendants and
Brandenburgs in silk passementerie.
UFAC collection, gift of Princess Joseph de Broglie, 1950,
inv. UF 50-6-5

**Blouson jacket
Popy Moreni, c. 1977**
Knotted stitch on canvas, knitted
garter stitch and woollen braid.
Gift of Mme Popy Moreni, 2005, inv. 2005.31.38
*One of the first pieces designed
by Popy Moreni, made by her mother*

154.
**Bustier dress
Carven, 1954–56**
Cotton with batik-style print.
UFAC collection, purchased, 1990, inv. UF 90-28-3

**Dress
Aux Trois Quartiers – Félix, 1908–10**
Satin with stripes of sabré velvet,
bodice in silk tulle and satin.
UFAC collection, purchased, 1992, inv. 92-17-3

**Visite coat
1870–80**
Black cashmere embroidered with
multicoloured floral motifs on a ground
of multicoloured checks, fringed edges,
bell sleeves, taffeta lining.
UFAC collection, gift of Pasquino, 1959, inv. 59-4-5

**Short tippet cape
Maison Decourt, 1895–1900**
Wool with stitched bands, grey
mother-of-pearl buttons,
turn-down collar in green velvet,
beige surah lining.
UFAC collection, gift of Ricaud, 1957, inv. 57-46-1

Spanish Style

The town of Arles is more Spanish than French. Bullfights, festivals, Spanish music drifting out of the houses like a collage of sound – all of these things are more than a tradition, they are part of everyday life. Paris definitely felt like a foreign country to me!

When I had to imagine what the fashion of 'Christian Lacroix' would look like, I naturally turned towards this idea of Spain that was both close and distant (I have not been there often).

This patchwork country, both pagan and Christian, sometimes with very British tastes (just compare its colourful prints with tartan), its rough jewels, its painters – Velázquez, Goya, Picasso – has been by my side in every collection, in the curves of strong, dark and sombre silhouettes, or quite the opposite, at the centre of a blazingly coloured motif.

In fashion, I admire the strictness of Spanish designers, who could all have become wonderful painters, just as the painters I mentioned could all have been fascinating couturiers, if they had only swapped their brushes for scissors. Balenciaga, Castillo, later Sybilla, they all developed a very pure style of sketching and an architectural precision but without denying the kitsch decoration that I love, creating a unique balance of artifice and fashion in their art.

Christian Lacroix Collection

156.
Haute Couture
Fall–Winter 1990–91
Model no. 34: *Sangre de Toro*
Red velvet bolero embroidered with
'Mantón de Manila' silk flowers.
Purple velvet gilet embroidered
with gold.
Tulip skirt in fuchsia-coloured
duchesse satin.
Christian Lacroix Archives

158 & 159.
Haute Couture
Fall–Winter 2003–4
Model no. 32
Long dress in flesh-coloured
creponné muslin with black printed
motifs; one frilled sleeve; the other
sleeve in shocking pink satin painted
with giant red and black flowers;
panel of black organdie printed with
large spots and smocked on one side,
and oversized blue organdie flounce
trimmed with black lace.
Christian Lacroix Archives

Les Arts Décoratifs, Mode et Textile Collection

160.
Evening dress
Jeanne Paquin, 1939
Silk velvet with integrated bands of silk
crêpe print with silver and gold lamé.
UFAC collection, gift of the Marquise de Paris,
1971, inv. 71-27-10 AB

Texture

Haute couture allows heights of sophistication to be reached that are not always or only dependent on the use of exceptional and expensive materials. To create original 'bespoke' fabrics, we reversed the stages of designing and constructing a dress or a suit, and followed the design and cutting with a stage involving skilled handweaving and fabric design.

By choosing to invent a palette in this way and create unique, unprecedented, unbridled materials, we were also renewing our link with far-off history, when weaving was done at a rate of 20 cm per day. What might nowadays be pejoratively referred to as a handicraft was turned into an exclusive luxury technique, through the skill of wonderful artisans.

It is no longer enough to make coats and suits with a fabric that has not been handworked as well as machine worked. To rediscover the most basic qualities of the material, tweed can be attacked, overstitched and extended with a sort of laser-cut muslin, frayed at the edges. In an era in which Lycra has received the blessing of fashion designers, we wanted to go back to fabrics as raw materials, reworking them like intricate lace and introducing the notion of time as the ultimate luxury.

162.
Haute Couture
Fall–Winter 2006–7
Model no. 37
Long dress entirely of lace and gold
braid in graduated shades
with an embroidered purple belt.
Christian Lacroix Archives

Haute Couture
Spring–Summer 2001
Model no. 9
Long jacket in hand-woven black
and white tweed with stencilled
flower appliqué.
Asymmetric blouse in fuchsia pink
and black striped organza over a
white gauze skirt with flat pleats
and decorative black stitching.
Christian Lacroix Archives

164.
Haute Couture
Fall–Winter 1997–98
Model no. 16
Short knitted jacket in Chantilly,
tulle and mohair in baby pink, dusky
pink and black with lace appliqué.
Matching skirt with flounced hem
and lace top.
Christian Lacroix Archives

Haute Couture
Spring–Summer 1995
Model no. 16
Belted suit in a mixed weave of
passementerie, macramé and lace
in shades of café au lait.
Christian Lacroix Archives

165.
Afternoon ensemble: miniskirt
and sailor top
Pierre Cardin Boutique, 1966
Wool and mohair mix tweed patterned
with white, beige, navy and turquoise
checks.
Taupe jersey top lined with matching
crêpe de Chine.
UFAC collection, gift of Mme Malitte Matta, 1978,
inv. 78-5-11 ABC

Suit
Chanel, Haute Couture Winter 1967,
fabric by Bucol
Pale green tweed mottled with pink and
grey, matching quilted lining, sleeveless
top in silk jersey and gold lurex with
green, violet and yellow stripes.
UFAC collection, gift of the house of Chanel, 1971,
inv. 71-30-16 ABC

166.
Evening ensemble: sheath dress
and jacket
Chanel, 1967
Metallic gold and silver lamé lined
with horizontally striped silk lamé
in yellow, pink and gold, cabochon
buttons in topaz and gold.
Gift of Chanel, 1976, inv. 76-29-20 AB

167.
Three-piece suit: evening jacket,
long skirt and slip
Kostio de War, c. 1933
Copper-coloured loose-weave knit
worn over gold lamé underdress.
Donated by Mme Georgette Camille, 1992, inv. 52807.A-C

168.
Cardigan
Sonia Delaunay, 1925–30
Woollen yarn in various shades of green,
edged with green braid.
Gift of M. Delaunay in memory of his mother,
Mme Sonia Delaunay, 1980, inv. 47700

Cardigan
Sonia Delaunay, 1925–30
Woollen yarn with dark red and grey
horizontal stripes, edged with braid
in the same shades.
Gift of M. Delaunay in memory of his mother,
Mme Sonia Delaunay, 1980, inv. 47699

Cardigan
Sonia Delaunay, 1925–30
Woollen yarn with horizontal stripes
in yellow, rust and green, striped
woollen braid in the same shades.
Gift of M. Delaunay in memory of his mother,
Mme Sonia Delaunay, 1980, inv. 47698

Gilet
Sonia Delaunay, 1925–30
Green woollen yarn, V-neck,
light green and yellow braid.
Gift of M. Delaunay in memory of his mother,
Mme Sonia Delaunay, 1980, inv. 47701

Cobwebs

My childhood is linked by moments of endless contemplation. I used to stare at things until I felt like I was inhabiting them from the inside. A tiled wall, a painting, an image, a bump in the floor, the corner of a cushion or a piece of wallpaper: anything could set me off on a new journey.

This may be why I'm so fond of the fantastic landscapes described by Victor Hugo, in which one could become lost forever.

From sketch to dress, from fabric to lace, thread is another running theme. It is both a motif and a form of writing; the bare bones of fashion, a glittering spider's web that has no wrong side or right side when it becomes a transparent dress.

CHRISTIAN LACROIX COLLECTION

170.
Haute Couture
Fall–Winter 2003–4
Model no. 20
Long asymmetric sheath dress in
black lace with a bronze painted
design and trimmings in red fur.

Christian Lacroix Archives

Haute Couture
Fall–Winter 1993–94
Model no. 34
Blouse in black Chantilly lace and
pleated muslin with tie fastening.
Long skirt with pleated black crêpe
flounce.

Christian Lacroix Archives

LES ARTS DÉCORATIFS, MODE ET TEXTILE COLLECTION

172.
Evening dress
Sonia Delaunay, 1926
Black silk tulle embroidered with silk
thread in pink, pale green and bright
blue, overstitched in gold.

UFAC collection, gift of Mme Sonia Delaunay, 1965, inv. 65-10-1

173.
Evening dress
Madeleine Vionnet, 1930–35
Black tulle decorated with horizontal
bands of gold lamé, bodice finished
with a small flounce at the neckline.

UFAC collection, gift of Mme Madeleine Vionnet, 1952,
inv. 52-18-852

174 & 175.
'Cage' coat
Elsa Schiaparelli, Summer 1937
Black mesh of horsehair yarn edged
with braid in the same material.

UFAC collection, gift of Mme Patricia Lopez-Willshaw,
1966, inv. 66-38-4 B

176.
Dress
c. 1937
Black machine-made net with a very
open weave and gathered flounces
in black silk tulle.

UFAC collection, gift of Abbadie d'Arrast, 1977, inv. 77-29-5

Dress
1920–30
Black silk string macramé with fringing.

UFAC collection, gift of Ramas, 1965, inv. 65-52-9

Art of the Unusual

My longstanding love of bad taste. This is what sends me with an unquenchable gusto into kitsch boutiques, towards Ferdinand Cheval's Palais Idéal or the seashell salt cellars of my youth.

The unique and singular nature of the folklore of daily life, popular culture and crafts is what allows them to reach the luxurious heights of haute couture.

In Villeneuve d'Ascq, on a visit to the Musée de l'Art Brut, I was stunned by a long dress created by a mental patient from the 1920s. Built from tiny pieces of material and so heavily embroidered on both sides that the threads formed a fabric in themselves, it was a startling work of textile art, a waking dream, a patched-together fantasy.

Haute couture should cling tightly to its obsession with the unusual and not forget about craftsmanship as the official source of magic in a discipline in which luxury does not always go hand in hand with financial means.

Tinfoil embroideries and jet beads, motifs made with marker pens and felt-tips and classic prints taken from sample books: I love them all.

178.
Haute Couture
Spring–Summer 2002
Model no. 8
Short jacket in white crêpe, decorated
with black lace and white fringing.
African-style tricolour sweater and short
skirt in black taffeta embroidered
with naive motifs in silver.
Christian Lacroix Archives

Haute Couture
Fall–Winter 2002–3
Model no. 19
Coat in a patchwork of coloured fur
with embroidered corselet.
Short dress in '*Hawaï*' painted silk,
with a taffeta bustier embroidered
and edged with fur on a ground of
black Chantilly lace.
Christian Lacroix Archives

180.
Haute Couture
Fall–Winter 1987–88
Model no. 51: *Sarah*
Coat dress in satin, '*Lola de Valence*'
hand-painted decoration.
Christian Lacroix Archives

181.
Long gown: *Deuxième robe de ville*
Jean Dubuffet, 1973
Satin crêpe, hand-painted abstract
decoration of sinuous black lines,
filled with red and blue blocks and
stripes, characteristic of Dubuffet's
Hourloupe cycle.
Gift of Mme Margit Rowell, 2006, inv. 2006.10.1

182 & 183.
Dress
Suzanne Conrard, c. 1925
Metallic mesh embroidered with wool
and mercerized cotton.
UFAC collection, gift of Mlle Suzanne Conrard, 1970, inv. 70-42-1

Dress
Suzanne Conrard, c. 1925
Cotton mesh embroidered with wool.
UFAC collection, gift of Mlle Suzanne Conrard, 1970, inv. 70-42-2

Dress
Suzanne Conrard, c. 1925
Golden square mesh, embroidered
with chenille motifs.
UFAC collection, gift of Mlle Suzanne Conrard, 1970, inv. 70-42-3

Tunic
Suzanne Conrard, c. 1925
Mesh, embroidered with wool and gold
braid motifs.
UFAC collection, gift of Mlle Suzanne Conrard, 1970, inv. 70-42-4

184.
Two-part dress with train
Desbuissons et Hudelist, 1900
Silk satin, embroidered with black and
steel sequins, jet beads, faille lining.
UFAC collection, gift of Mme Strohl, 1953, inv. 53-10-1 AB

Jacket
Elsa Schiaparelli, Winter 1937–38,
embroidery by Maison Lesage
Wool, embroidered with gold thread,
pearls and cut stones.
UFAC collection, gift of Mme Patricia Lopez-Willshaw,
1966, inv. 66-38-12

Evening jacket
1905–10,
embroidery by Maison Rébé
Wool with silk velvet appliqué,
embroidered with jet beads,
sequins and braid, satin lining.
Gift of M. Rébé, embroiderer, 1974, inv. 44811

185.
Skirt
Clergeat, 1898–1900
Silk satin, embroidered with wood, gold
and transparent sequins, frill in ecru lace,
chiffon, cream taffeta lining.
UFAC collection, gift of Mlle Solange Granet, 1966,
inv. 66-40-3 AB

186.
Dress
Lola Prusac, 1960
Knitted from raffia, silk cord and gold
lamé on a base of woven canvas ribbon.
UFAC collection, gift of Mme Lola Prusac, 1981, inv. 81-6-2

Dress
Lola Prusac, 1960–63
Knitted from multicoloured wool and
gold lamé on a tulle base.
UFAC collection, gift of Mme Lola Prusac, 1980, inv. 81-6-3

Dress
Christian Dior by Marc Bohan, c. 1967
Wool crêpe, appliqué decoration of
metallic Rhodoid and satin stitch in wool.
Gift of Mme Hélène David-Weill, 1997, inv. 997.47.20.1

187.
Coat
c. 1920
Silk velvet embroidered with brass thread
and gold glass beads.
Gift of M. Patrick Cartoux, 1997, inv. 997.53.1

Evening gown
Jacques Doucet, c. 1927
Silk crêpe, embroidered with glass beads
and gold thread in satin stitch.
Gift of M. Al. Laidley, 1986, inv. 58346

Evening gown
1920–25
Georgette crêpe, with crêpe de chine
appliqué and gold embroidery
in raised satin stitch, draped petal
skirt with tulle edging.
UFAC collection, gift of Mlle G. Lecuyer-Corthis, 1953,
inv. 53-32-3

The Forgotten Couturier

In the 1970s, during a trip to the US, I discovered the work of Mainbocher, a French and later American couture house, founded in 1929.

Main Rousseau Bocher began his career selling illustrations for *Vogue* and *Harper's Bazaar* before becoming editor in chief of French *Vogue*. He was the first American to open a couture house in Paris and his success was immediate.

Wallis Simpson, the Duchess of Windsor, was one of his most famous clients and hired him to make her wedding gown.

His evening dresses, with their pure, refined lines, changed the silhouette of the times. They suited a new clientele of adventurous women who seemed less stuffy and more modern.

His way of using embroidery as a fabric in itself was striking. Long dresses with tube sleeves, collarless and almost austere, had a visionary simplicity that anticipated the 1960s, although they were designed in the 1930s. Floral or geometric embroidered fabrics in a range of pastel or blazing shades awakened in me the insatiable taste for colours that I had as a child.

Mainbocher was a past master in the art of twisting the use of materials, creating evening gowns from men's shirt fabric. He could also produce sports jackets or day outfits from silky fabrics that were generally used for eveningwear.

This short tartan dress with its bodice embroidered with scattered flowers, these gowns that glide over the body like gem-studded paintings seem to my eyes to represent the ultimate in elegance.

CHRISTIAN LACROIX COLLECTION

190.
Haute Couture
Spring–Summer 1998
Model no. 38
Long Maharani sheath dress
in mauve and cornflower blue
organza covered in embroidery.
Christian Lacroix Archives

Haute Couture
Fall–Winter 1999–2000
Model no. 32
Long mosaic sheath dress in red,
orange, aniseed green and black vinyl.
Christian Lacroix Archives

LES ARTS DÉCORATIFS, MODE ET TEXTILE COLLECTION

192 & 193.
Evening dress
Mainbocher, Summer 1937
Black tulle embroidered with rectangular
sequins in red, green, violet and blue.
UFAC collection, gift of M. Main R. Bocher, 1961, inv. 61-19-19

Evening dress
Mainbocher, 1937
Black tulle embroidered with
multicoloured sequins.
UFAC collection, gift of M. Main R. Bocher, 1961, inv. 61-19-17

194.
Evening dress
Mainbocher, 1936
Silver lamé embroidered
with green beads.
UFAC collection, gift of M. Main R. Bocher, 1961, inv. 61-19-6

Evening dress
Mainbocher, 1936
Pink silk crêpe with appliqué green
bands, embroidered all over with gold,
pink and green beads.
UFAC collection, gift of M. Main R. Bocher, 1961, inv.61-19-2

Elsewhere

I used to constantly ask my family and others around me about what it was like 'before'; I wanted to know about the gestures, the smells, the colours. Other places are closely related to other times. Both give a status to history and both play a part in my concept of it.

I don't recognize the virtues that others find in travel, and remain satisfied with the diluted images that come right into my room, at a time when all the world's barriers have fallen.

By contrast, I am always captivated by the anachronism or the geographic miracle that occurs when a Tibetan hat turns up on a market stall in London or Madrid. The series of exotic influences that fashion has soaked up throughout the 20th century have transformed the way we dress into a tangible map of the world. From Paul Poiret, that sultan among couturiers, to Mariano Fortuny, with his longing for the ancient world, from Jeanne Lanvin, lover of Slavic embroidery, to Elsa Schiaparelli, creator of all kinds of cross-bred combinations, fashion can be inspired by all regions, all countries, without ever falling into mere folklore.

If there must be folklore, it ought to be contemporary, emerging from the powerhouse of the city, which both feeds imaginations and allows the co-existence of different worlds, the coming together of strangers who would never have met.

Everything that interests me in folk art as a mirror of a region or land can be found in the interminglings of urban life. The original sources seem far away to me. I prefer combinations, the wanderings and gatherings of gypsies who carried with them treasures more captivating than we can emulate, like hunters with their trophies. I love the way that they dress themselves in the relics of other places.

Rather than the frenetic travel our society is obsessed with, I prefer the approach taken by Des Esseintes in Huysmans's novel *À rebours*; en route to England, he decides to end his journey at the Gare du Nord, where the pubs already feel more like London than Paris.

196.
Haute Couture
Spring–Summer 2002
Model no. 14
Short-sleeved ecru tulle blouse with
lace appliqué, worn with a white silk
gilet in Boutis embroidery.
Roughly pleated skirt in white
organdie with tulle apron with
Directoire-style embroidery.
Christian Lacroix Archives

Haute Couture
Spring–Summer 1994
Model no. 18
Knit bolero in burgundy and bronze
with tie fastening.
Red silk t-shirt with floral print.
Pyjama trousers with Provençal
pattern in a graduated red/yellow
colour scheme, belted with a shawl
in coordinating stripes.
Christian Lacroix Archives

198.
Visite coat
1870–80
Black cashmere, embroidered with
multicoloured silk, decorated with
multicoloured braids and fringing
in silk, bell sleeves, black silk lining.
UFAC collection, gift of Mme Fabre, 1962, inv. 62-19-1

199.
'Lido' bolero
Claude Saint-Cyr, Winter 1951
Needlepoint on a silk base by the Atelier
Pinton from a design by François Adnet,
black silk grosgrain lining.
Acquired through the patronage of Mrs Jayne Wrightsman,
2001, inv. 2001.134.1.1

Short coat
Claude Saint-Cyr, Winter 1951
Needlepoint on a wool base by
the Atelier Pinton from a design by
Georges Martin, lining in quilted beige
silk grosgrain, with decorative stitching.
Acquired through the patronage of Mrs Jayne Wrightsman, 2001,
inv. 2001.134.2

Short coat
Claude Saint-Cyr, Winter 1951
Needlepoint on a wool base by the
Atelier Pinton from a design by Georges
Martin, lining in quilted beige silk
grosgrain, with decorative stitching.
Acquired through the patronage of Mrs Jayne Wrightsman, 2001,
inv. 2001.134.3

200.
Dress
c. 1910
Pale pink calico, white calico bib
sprigged with red flowers, pink braid,
embroidered tulle, lawn embroidered in
satin stitch and insertion of handmade
and machine lace.
UFAC collection, gift of Mlle Andrée Frantz-Jourdain, 1963,
inv. 63-12-174

Dress
c. 1910
Pale pink calico, white calico bib
sprigged with red flowers, pink braid,
embroidered tulle, lawn embroidered in
satin stitch and insertion of handmade
and machine lace.
UFAC collection, gift of Mlle Andrée Frantz-Jourdain, 1963,
inv. 63-12-175

Coat
Paul Poiret, 1910-15
Cherry red grosgrain, net trim
embroidered with a relief pattern in
white cotton, facings and lining in black
satin, Brandenburgs and gilt buttons.
UFAC collection, gift of Mme Bonnard, 1961, inv. 61-40-1

201.
Cape
Caroline Reboux, 1935
Silk satin with decorative appliqué.
UFAC collection, gift of Mme Lucienne Rabate, 1956,
inv. 56-62-112 bis

Cape
Caroline Reboux, 1935
Crêpe romain with decorative appliqué.
UFAC collection, gift of Mme Lucienne Rabate, 1956,
inv. 56-62-121

Cape
Caroline Reboux, 1935
Crêpe romain with decorative appliqué.
UFAC collection, gift of Mme Lucienne Rabate, 1956,
inv. 56-62-118

202.
Dress
c. 1915
Pale grey crêpe romain and chiffon, trimmed with beaded wool net.
UFAC collection, gift of Mme Le Bec, 1969, inv. 69-26-13

Dress
Jean Patou, 1920–25
White chiffon with print motif in beige, red and black and trimmed with a black satin band, beige silk underdress.
UFAC collection, gift of Mme François de Saxcé, 1984, inv. 84-16-19 AB

Tunic dress
Nicole Groult, 1920–25
Black marocain decorated with white silk machine embroidery, sleeves lined with orange crêpe de Chine.
UFAC collection, gift of Mme Margaritis, 1968, inv. 68-17-1

203.
Sleeveless gilet
Sonia Delaunay, 1924
Navy blue wool with multicoloured needlepoint embroidery in wool, navy corozo buttons and lining of navy satin.
UFAC collection, gift of Mme Sonia Delaunay, 1965, inv. 65-10-4

Jacket
Paul Poiret, 1920s
Ivory wool embroidered with Romanian motifs in blue and black wool, in satin stitch, herringbone stitch, cross stitch and couching.
UFAC collection, gift of Baroness Gourgaud, 1959, inv. UF 59-7-2

Top
1920–25
Ivory-coloured flannel, round neckline in navy-blue wool with turquoise chevrons, long sleeves in black and white striped wool, small white buttons on the shoulders.
UFAC collection, gift of Mme Elvire Popesco, 1956, inv. 56-6-21

204.
Afternoon dress
Nicole Groult, c. 1910
Green crêpe de Chine sheath dress, white crepon tunic with a band of white cotton net embroidered in coloured silks, belt and trimmings in pink taffeta with green fringing.
UFAC collection, gift of M. Marcel Piccioni, 1970, inv. 70-38-17

Tunic
c. 1925
Black silk jersey edged with a bias-cut band of sky blue crêpe de Chine, decorative appliqué in pink and blue crêpe de Chine.
UFAC collection, gift of Mme Hélène Brès-Chouanard, 1975, inv. 75-7-111

205.
Jacket
Sonia Delaunay, 1924, model no. 1
Yellow cotton, decorated with needlepoint embroidery, edged with chestnut silk crêpe.
UFAC collection, gift of Mme Sonia Delaunay, 1965, inv. 65-10-2

Blouse
Louise Boulanger, c. 1926
Orange-red silk crêpe with painted decoration by Jean Dunand.
UFAC collection, gift of Mme Agnès, 1949, inv. 49-6-5

Shawl collar
Sonia Delaunay, 1925–30
Wool with ikat-effect chevron motif.
Gift of M. Delaunay, in memory of his mother, Mme Sonia Delaunay, 1980, inv. 47694

Bolero
Sonia Delaunay, 1925–30
Natural linen, printed with woodcut motifs in two colours, short turned-up sleeves with plain linen cuffs.
Gift of M. Delaunay, in memory of his mother, Mme Sonia Delaunay, 1980, inv. 47692

Of all the plays whose costumes have influenced my haute couture work, *Othello* is undoubtedly the most obvious. As I delved into archives of antique clothing, second-hand shops, army surplus stores, in search of darker shades, I ended up imagining new but ragged clothes, chic hybrids, in tints ranging from wine to charcoal.

The use of black preceded the use of colour, in both my sketches and my clothes, although my love of colour is all that is ever mentioned. Black lines outline a silhouette on paper before the choice of fabrics brings it to life.

To me, black is the opposite of minimalism, I like infinite blacks, those that are bleached by the sun and by time, matte blacks, glossy blacks, opulent blacks. The blacks used by Spanish painters, of course, but also those of northern painters such as Hals. Black radicalizes and dramatizes. Chanel's little black dress from 1927 or the castaway black of the Japanese designers whose runway shows I discovered in the early 1980s, these things are breaking points in fashion, milestones and anchoring places.

Rather than flat expanses of black, I prefer ribbons, ruches, holes, depth that can be sculpted, adding shadow to the darkness.

If my work has a Mediterranean influence, it appears in black as well as in colour. Its solemn, dramatic side can be seen in the black sable of *Vulcano*, in the jet-black hair and austere wardrobe of the stunning Anna Magnani, in the ritualistic style and haughty posture of the women of Arles, in black statues of the Virgin, in the garb of mourning whose sombre shades tinted the 19th century.

208.
Haute Couture
Fall–Winter 1987–88
Model no. 1: *Marie*
Suit in quilted black silk
with embroidered sleeves.
Christian Lacroix Archives

Haute Couture
Fall–Winter 2006–7
Model no. 9
Doublet-style jacket in black crêpe
with a bodice embroidered with
graduating jet beads, and a sunshine
yellow taffeta bow brooch on
the nape of the neck.
Short skirt of ruffled black taffeta
over an embroidered lace underskirt.
Christian Lacroix Archives

210.
Black evening skirts and tops
Jeanne Lanvin, 1935
Crêpe de Chine, embroidered
with overlapping sequins.
UFAC collection, gift of Mlle Nadia Boulanger, 1990,
inv. 90-52-20 AB

Baby doll dress
Balenciaga, 1958
Black machine-made lace
with black satin bows.
UFAC collection, purchased, 1988, inv. 88-11-3

Suit
Christian Dior Boutique, 1950s
Knopped wool and ribbed knit in black
mohair, lining in ivory silk taffeta.
Gift of Princess Schonburg, 1994, inv. 994.111.1.AB

Two-piece '*Londres***' dress**
Christian Dior, Fall–Winter 1950
Wool serge, turn-down collar above
a triangular opening with a row
of four buttons on either side.
UFAC collection, gift of Mme Hélène Brès-Chouanard, 1975,
inv. 75-7-622 bis AB

211.
Evening dress
Madeleine Vionnet, 1918
Black silk tulle with a very open weave,
trimmed with narrow satin ribbon.
UFAC collection, gift of Mme Madeleine Vionnet, 1952,
inv. 52-18-3

Evening dress
Attributed to Maggy Rouff, c. 1935
Ciré satin.
UFAC collection., anonymous gift, 1966, inv. 66-12-3

Evening dress
c. 1900
Figured black tulle covered with
black sequins and lined in black taffeta,
collarette of black sequins, ruffles
of black silk tulle.
UFAC collection, gift of M. and Mme Wormser, 1972, inv. 72-10-1

Cape and long dress
Yves Saint Laurent,
Fall–Winter 1988–99
Double thickness cloqué, black lamé,
lined with fuchsia pink satin,
dress in the same satin
Gift of the house of Yves Saint Laurent, 1998, inv. 998.39.41.1-2

212&213.
Suit
Christian Dior, 1949
Ribbed black wool serge, black silk
velvet, black corozo buttons,
narrow belt in black suede.
UFAC collection, gift of Mrs Kaindl, 1971, inv. 71-37-6 ABC

Afternoon dress
Lucien Lelong, 1945–48
Black wool crêpe with slit neckline.
UFAC collection, gift of Mme Maurice Goudeket, 1970,
inv. 70-10-4

Evening dress
Charles Frederick Worth, c. 1895
Cut velvet on satin foundation.
Gift of Mme Franklin Gordon Dexter, 1920, inv. 22014.A

Mourning dress
Ch. Drecoll, c. 1915
Wool serge, the glossiness
of the ribbon accentuating
the matte effect of the dress.
Purchased, 1996, inv. 996.71.1

Long jacket
Maggy Rouff, 1890–1900
Black silk velvet with jet embroidery,
stiffened inner bodice in beige faille,
black silk lining.
UFAC collection, gift of Mme Muller, 1958, inv. 58-39-2

214.
Evening coat
Jeanne Lanvin, 1935
Black marocain, patch pockets
covered in rabbit fur.
Gift of Mme Brigitte de Lacretelle, 1993, inv. 993.104.1

Tunic
1920s
Georgette crêpe trimmed
with cord and tassel.
Gift of Mme Failliot-Bournisien, 1990, inv. 990.933 A

Tunic
1920s
Georgette crêpe trimmed
with cord and tassel.
Gift of Mme Failliot-Bournisien, 1990, inv. 990.933 B

Sketchbook

moyen
âge

valois

Louis
XIII

Louis
XVI

Regence

Louis XV

The History of Fashion
Computer-generated sketches
Christian Lacroix, 2007

Like my favourite childhood toy for many years, those sets of cards divided into three (heads, bodies and legs) that can be endlessly interchanged, the history of fashion is an unruly combination of different eras, in which the end of one can be seen in the shape of a sleeve, and the beginning of the next in the curve of a bodice.

As a child, from the age of six, I used to love drawing each one of these changes, building up big historical friezes. As well as including representations of the costume of every decade from the 17th century to the present day or from different regions, I wanted to note down and pinpoint every change in fashion, however tiny. I never seemed to stop expanding this catalogue of exhaustive and frivolous details. This understanding lies at the very heart of my designs.

Louis
XVI

Revolu-
tion

1820

1830

1860

1880

1900   1915   1920   1930   1938   '60

Fall–Winter 2007–8
Haute Couture collection
Computer-generated sketches
Christian Lacroix, 2007

The neverending cycle of returning fashions, limited at the start of the 18th century, regular in the 19th century and rapid throughout the 20th century, is probably the best definition of fashion history, with couture clothes taking the place of historical costumes. The creation of the Fall–Winter 2007–8 Haute Couture collection, at a time when the house was celebrating its 20th anniversary, is proof of the permanence and influence of the history of fashion and costume in my work. More inexpressible than in my school exercise books, fashion history is the common blueprint behind all my collections. Before I became a couturier, as I catalogued every development in fashion evolution, I liked to imagine the possibility of making things modern and yet still maintaining the distinctive marks of a particular era. Now this need has become an intoxicating natural high, imprinted on the designs and the fabrics of every collection.

G'2'

sans
plume
finalement

234